# A POCKET FULL

# OF

# STONES

Small Nuggets to Help You Create
Big Change

## KEVIN MCNEIL

*Thanks Kevin*

*Blessings*

*You,*

www.thetwelveproject.com

# **Contents**

# The Pursuit of Happiness

*Because I'm Happy*

*Clap along if you feel like a room without a roof*

*Because I'm happy*

*Clap along if you feel like happiness is the truth*

*Because I'm happy*

*Clap along if you know what happiness is to you*

*Because I'm happy*

*Clap along if you feel like that's what you wanna do*

*Pharell*

Can I ask you a personal question?

Are you happy? This question doesn't require much thought. It can be answered with either a "Yes" or a "No." But in truth the answer to this question will depend on how you define happiness. So, maybe I should ask the question differently. Let's try this one. What is happiness and where do you find it? Now, that's better. This question cannot be answered with a simple yes or no. Ask someone to define happiness and they will probably describe a life without problems. Some people may say wealth brings happiness. These people think money is the answer to all life's problems. However, we all know that not to be true. Someone may answer that "being healthy is what brings happiness." To them, a life without health problems sounds like a form of happiness. Some may be convinced that finding true love will make someone live happily ever after. These people really want a relationship without pain or disappointment. The bottom line is that we don't like problems. We spend most of our lives avoiding problems; thinking this will bring us happiness. If we are going to be successful we must change the way we view problems. In fact, we must forget about being happy.

Is happiness really the absence of problems? We all know that inevitably life is full of problems. No one gets through life without any problems. Now I know you thought you were the only one with problems. Sorry to break the news to you, but we all have problems. In fact, we need problems. Imagine a life without problems. Happiness, right? Wrong! Life would be boring. We would still be living a primitive lifestyle. Every invention or advancement in our world was due to someone attempting to solve a problem. If we didn't have problems there would be no computers, airplanes, or cell phones. Scary, huh? Especially the no cell phone part. We would have no automobiles, paved roads, or Starbucks. Now, that would be a problem. Our world is a result of people solving problems, not searching for happiness. Problems do not produce unhappiness nor does the lack of problems produce happiness. Happiness is not found. It is created by solving a problem. Problems are opportunities to create happiness. This is why the most successful people in our world are problem solvers not happiness seekers. So, if you are not getting what I am trying to say; let me say it more clearly: *Overcoming problems is what produces happiness. You will never be happy avoiding problems.* Okay! Maybe I wasn't clear enough, so I will say it louder:

YOU NEED PROBLEMS TO BE HAPPY.

### What are problems?

> *"Problems are not stop signs, they are guidelines."*
> Robert Schuller

Before we continue, let me clarify what I am referring to as problems. I am not referring to the problems we create. I am talking about life's problems. Problems are a part of life. Only dead people don't have to deal with life's problems. I am talking about people-created problems or the problems we create. Often the problems we create come from us attempting to avoid life's problems. For instance, everyone desires to be in a loving relationship. However, any relationship is going to have its own set of problems. Like you, the person whom you involve yourself with has a personal history. Perhaps you were raised in a single parent home, while your mate grew up in a loving two parent household. This variance may cause you both to look at life differently. This can cause challenges to arise at some point in the relationship. These challenges do not come to destroy the relationship but to strengthen it. The goal is to understand each other while working through whatever problem that arises. However, instead of working through the problem some people may seek quick solutions. They might say they are unhappy in the relationship. They view the problem as the source of their unhappiness. So, they attempt to solve the problem. Their idea of a solution may be to look for happiness elsewhere, which could involve having an affair. The affair may bring temporary excitement, but later causes another problem: infidelity. When the spouse finds out about the affair it causes distrust, and that is a problem you created. This was a problem you created to avoid the original (life) problem. The original problem could have strengthened the relationship, if solved responsibly and cohesively. However, because you simply wanted to be happy, you sought a quick solution. The long-term solution would have been to recognize the problem and discuss it. Happiness is not the real goal. The goal is building a stronger relationship. Many people think they want to be happy. Really, it is not happiness they seek, it is a life without problems. The pursuit of happiness is what actually causes unhappiness. Why are we so preoccupied with happiness? I am happy you asked.

**Unhappy in Paradise**

> *Paradise: a place of extreme beauty, delight, or happiness; a state of supreme happiness; bliss.* Dictionary.com

The search for happiness is as old as civilization itself. The first two humans are said to have lived in paradise, and still they were not happy. They had food, security, and good health. But they felt they were missing one thing: happiness. Adam and Eve were never promised happiness. God told them to be *fruitful and multiply.* How were they to accomplish this task?

They were to be responsible with what they were given. Adam and Eve missed this important lesson; *they were not created to be happy.* Neither were we. We were created to be fruitful. Fruitful means to be problem solvers. God gave the first humans a garden and told them to cultivate it. In other words, they were given an unsolved problem. The garden (problem) had potential, but it needed God's power to produce life. I hope you catch the revelation. Humankind was created to become vessels of God's power, not to be happy. God blesses us with purpose, so we can solve problems. God will direct you to your purpose by giving you an unsolved problem. If you run from these problems, you will never discover your purpose. Again, your purpose is tied to a problem. You and I were born to turn problems into life-giving solutions. How do you live a successful life? Stop searching for happiness and start looking for the specific problem God created you to solve.

The first thing God gives humankind after giving them life is responsibility. Why? Because life is about responsibility. Adam and Eve's responsibility was the same as God's when he created heaven and earth: prepare the environment to bring forth life. Don't miss this crucial point; *we were created to bring forth life.*

Instead they brought forth death. How? They did so by making happiness their goal. Their search for happiness made them forgo their responsibility. As a result, they were evicted from the Garden of Eden, their place of responsibility. Just like that, the search for happiness began. Centuries later we are still looking to be happy. We believe happiness exist somewhere out there. Our lives are spent looking for the right place to find it. We attend church, go to school, and get jobs because we want to be happy. Happiness is considered a hidden treasure. When we can't find it, we try to buy it. People get into large amount of debt buying things they believe will bring them happiness. Happiness is such a hot commodity people try to sell it to us. Have you ever tried to buy happiness?

The next time you watch a television commercial listen for the promise to make you happy: lawyers promise to get you the largest settlement possible, colleges promise you will soar in your career by getting a degree, food commercials assert their food will bring you bliss, weight loss commercials promise to help you look your best, and lottery advertisements tell you one dollar could change your life forever. Television commercials *do not sell products*, they sell happiness.

Television commercials are not the only purveyors of happiness. Companies hire celebrities to sell their products to convince us we too can be successful.

Type *books on happiness* into Google and thousands of results come up. We can even hear people try to encourage us to be happy in our music.

## The Sound of Happiness

Anytime I want to relax I put on some soft music and grab a nice book. Music is a universal language; it speaks to our hearts. It bypasses our thinking brain and goes straight to our emotional brain. The right song can send us down memory lane and make us forget all about our problems; especially a song called *Happy*. In 2014, music producer and artist Pharrell produced a song called *Happy*. The song took the world by storm.

Everyone produced their own happiness videos and posted them to social media. The refrain of the song, which simply says *"Because I'm Happy,"* reminded me of an old American fairytale, *The Little Engine that Could*. *The Little Engine that Could* was created to teach children about the power of optimism and believing in one's self. The story is about a train with a small engine carrying a heavy load of toys and foods. The train attempts to get toys and food over a hill to anxious awaiting little boys and girls.

In the middle of the journey, the small engine lost power and could no longer continue the journey. The little engine became sad. It wanted to get the toys and food to the awaiting boys and girls. Bigger trains passed by the little train. The little engine begged the bigger engines to help it get its cars over the hill. All the bigger engines made fun of the little engine and refused to help. After a while, this little blue engine strengthened up and pulled them over the hill. As the little blue engine strained up the hill, it repeated to itself, *"I think I can, I think I can, I think I can."* The train changed its mindset. As a result, the little train was able to get the toys and food to the children on the other side of the hill. Everyone lived happily ever after. Although everyone was happy, happiness was not his original goal. The goal was to overcome a problem to bring joy to other people.

However, unlike the fairytale, we can't chant or shout our way to happiness. Just like the little train, we must work to overcome our problems. The next time you hear a success story don't listen for the happy moments, listen for the problems the person or the company overcame. Watch how their faces light up when they explain how they kept believing in themselves despite their problems.

Happiness is the result of conquering, not avoiding problems.

# Don't Avoid Problems, Find a Challenge

In the above story, the little blue train did not see the hill as a problem, but instead as a challenge. You too must adopt this mindset. Strive to look at problems not as something to be avoided, but as challenges to be accepted. When we attempt to avoid problems, we create unhappiness. Problems sets off alarms in our brains. They tell our brains, *Hey! Pay attention, this is important*. If we treat a problem as a life-improving challenge, the brain gets to work to assist us in solving the problem. However, when we tell our brain that the problem is a threat, our brains switch into survival mode and start attacking the problem. As a result, the brain starts releasing stress hormones. These stress hormones make us feel unsafe, which then leads us to force ourselves away from problems rather than facing them head-on. Now, the thing that could have made us better has become the very thing we agonize over. Unhappiness comes from our mindset about the problem, not from the problem itself. Ask someone why they are unhappy, and they will give you several reasons. They may say they are lonely, overweight, broke, unemployed, or working in a dead-end job. Notice everything the person named are not actually problems; they are only challenges. It is this unwillingness to face the challenges in life that make people unhappy. What challenge are you facing right now? Is it the source of your unhappiness? What if you decided to do something about the so-called problem that is challenging your happiness? Okay, I didn't want to say this so bluntly, but I feel like it's necessary: You are your own problem!

If you still reading, I am happy. If not, we have a problem. Nope, it's not my book - it is still you. I did not write this book to make you happy. I wrote it to challenge you. So, let me reiterate, *happiness is not the absence of problems.* In fact, overcoming problems can provide us with fulfillment. Overcoming a problem can actually make us feel better. Let me give you an example: *You are sitting at home watching television on your nice, cozy living room couch. A television commercial comes on showing a homeless child sleeping under a bridge. You suddenly feel uneasy. You love children and wished there was something you could do. But wait, the announcer tells you there is something you can do to help the child. You can send in a donation that will give the child a meal and shelter for a week.*

*You don't have much money, but they are only asking for a small amount. So, you pick up the phone and donate. After, you hang up the phone you continue to eat your meal and watch your movie. When you lay down to go to bed your eyes glance up at your ceiling. You give God thanks for allowing you to have food and shelter. You wake up the next morning and find you are in a great mood. You head off to work and have a productive day.* What happened? You happened. Solving a problem made you happy. A minor problem engaged your heart. By giving to a charity or helping a homeless person we feel a sense of accomplishment. By giving to the charity we feel we have helped solve a universal problem. Why does this make us feel good? Because God created us to help others solve problems and make the world better. When we solve problems for others, we feel good. Don't miss the *"for others"* part.

When we focus on our own problems the brain sees it as a threat and releases stress hormones. When we focus on someone else's problem the brain views it as a challenge. In fact, the brain releases a feel-good hormone called dopamine when it experiences something novel or challenging. If you want to feel better, find a problem in the world to solve. It must be stimulating or challenging. Now, this does not mean it has to be big or important. It just has to be big or important to you. What is something that is close to your heart? It may be something you are currently struggling with right now; for the small act to feel big it must matter to you. The brain doesn't release this feel-good chemical if it doesn't find what you are doing challenging. Activities like skydiving, waterskiing, or ziplining give people an adrenaline rush or a dopamine high. All these activities challenge the brain's desire to keep you safe. People who do these activities overcome the brain's fear system. They accomplish this by reframing the activity as a challenge rather than a threat. You must do the same if you are going to be successful. Don't give to be happy; give to make a difference. Making a positive impact in the world is what brings happiness and success. Happiness and money are not synonymous. You don't need money to be happy. Find small ways to make a difference in the world and it will take your mind off your problems. Small things done with purpose give you a sense of accomplishment. I encourage you to think BIG and ACT small. If you want momentous change, I recommend you focus on the little things.

# All Things Start Small

*"Big things come in small packages."*

Although popular, few of us actually believe this statement. We abhor small things. We desire the big things in life, and in a world where big is everyone's goal, we often ignore the little things. We cherish big cars, huge houses, and people with massive bank accounts. However, I have discovered that big things really do come in small packages. Success consists of capitalizing on minor events that might seem unimportant at first. I've learned that everything starts off from a small seed, from babies to oak trees. Once I stopped chasing the big stuff and paid attention to the small, my life changed drastically for the better. I want to share with you some of these small things that made a big impact in my life. This book is about how to use small steps to make big changes in life. Big problems often start out small, like falling into debt (one dollar at a time), becoming overweight (one pound at a time), or getting into trouble (one bad decision at a time). In fact, few things start off big. A large oak tree grows from a small acorn; human beings start as a single cell; a dollar consists of one hundred pennies; and enormous breakthroughs often come from a tiny spark of an idea. If you want to be successful, aim big but focus small.

*"If you have faith as small as a mustard seed, you can say to this mulberry tree, 'Be uprooted and planted in the sea,' and it will obey you."* Luke 17:6 NIV

Like many of you, I have always yearned for success, and it seemed to elude me no matter how hard I tried to pursue my dreams. I spent years complaining and listening to my friends complain about life. When nothing else worked, I turned to religion. I thought the church would offer me hope, but people in church also complained about the difficulty of life. Religious leaders told me I lacked faith. So, I decided to get serious about my faith. I wanted to study God's word and find out what He or She wanted me to do with my life. I enrolled in seminary and applied to become a minister. After years of attending church and almost two hundred thousand dollars in student loan debt, I still had not found success. Success evaded me at every turn. There had to be more I could do. I figured I was not thinking big enough. I needed to make a big move and leap out into the unknown. It seemed to me that it was time for a big, drastic change to correct the large mistakes I had made. So I left the church and turned to motivational speaking and considered becoming a life coach. I got online and searched for every motivational conference I could find. My frequent flyer miles grew as I flew across the country looking for my big breakthrough. I spent thousands of dollars attending motivational speaking conferences. I joined several get-rich-quick pyramid schemes. I purchased and read every self-help book on the shelves. It still wasn't enough. No matter what I did, I felt stuck. My life was a drag. I felt like a giant failure. Then, one day, my prayers were answered. It didn't come in some big epiphany. I wasn't prophesied to or given a big revelation. My answer came while I was moping around with my head hanging down, looking at the ground. My big break *came in the most unlikely way and at the most inopportune time.*

## Little Things Add Up!

I pulled into the police precinct parking lot on an early Monday morning. I was tired. After eighteen years of doing police work, I wanted a change. I sat in my car, took a deep breath, and said a quick prayer. I felt guilty for complaining about my job. I had something most people dreamed of all their lives; a meaningful career. After pulling my thoughts together, I apologized and told God I was thankful to have a job. I sat in my unmarked car and watched people walk into the office building., wondering, *"Are all these people as unhappy as I am?"* A message chime on my phone reminded me I was running five minutes behind. I quickly grabbed my belongings and swung open the door. As I exited my patrol vehicle I saw a shiny object on the ground. Looking closely, I noticed it was a dime. I reluctantly picked it up and placed it in my pocket. I didn't want to just leave a shiny new dime on the ground. As I approached the door to my office building, I noticed another coin on the ground. This time it was a penny. I thought, *"Woohoo! Today is my lucky day!"* Finally, as I got on the elevator, another copper object on the floor caught my attention. I picked it up and proceeded to my office with a whopping twelve cents. As I contemplated what I was going to do with my newfound riches, a thought entered my mind: *"Honor the little things!"* That was strange. Random thoughts don't enter my mind often, so I contemplated what this meant, considering its gravity. Maybe it was a message from God. But why would God ask me to honor little things? I grew up thinking God wanted me to be great! Confused, I reached for my Bible, which was collecting dust on my desk, and opened it. As I read some familiar biblical scriptures, a pattern emerged. I noticed God chose seemingly unexceptional people to accomplish great feats. He chose a runaway fugitive to be a liberator, a shepherd boy to be a king, and a carpenter to be the savior of humanity. Although insignificant to others, these three were big in God's eyes. But why? The answer surprised me. I discovered what these men had in common is that they were responsible for things others thought were insignificant. This also held true for women in the Bible. The woman with the issue of blood touched the bottom of Jesus' robe, Rehab hid some Israelite spies, and Mary, the mother of Jesus, kept her pregnancy a secret. All these stories highlight how God honored those who were faithful in the smallest tasks. But it was the story of David that had the biggest impact on me. David's story stood out to me because he – literally a small, regular man - fought and defeated a giant. I was impressed with his courage to face such an intimidating warrior. As someone who was bullied all his life, I wished I had the courage to stand up to my enemies like David did. David was small in stature but did not fear anything. His courage made him fit to be a king. After careful examination, I discovered it wasn't his courage but his handling of seemingly minor things that prepared him for the position of king. He cared for and was prepared to sacrifice his life for his father's sheep. He ran unwanted errands for his family. He did the things no one else wanted to do. He did not complain, but was faithful. So, it is no surprise when God needed someone to accomplish something big, He chose someone who honored these little things. I began to realize why I was so unhappy. It wasn't that I didn't have a good life. I was ignoring what I considered insignificant things in my life. I didn't pay attention to how I spent my time, my money, or my influence. All the things I took for granted, God saw as important. As a result, every problem I had seemed relatively enormous. Because I ignored what I considered to be trivial things, everything in my life seemed like a Goliath. I began to wonder if behind all the big stories in the bible there were small hidden principles. I contemplated if following these same principles in this ancient text could make a big difference in our lives today. My curiosity led me to read scripture differently. More importantly, I began to see the world differently.

## Seeing for the First Time

I stood facing the mirror, half dressed, debating whether to call in sick yet again. My job as an officer was rewarding. I loved my job as a special victims' detective working child abuse cases. We did great work for families and their children. The job was also very challenging. Dealing with abuse can take its toll on anyone, especially a detective dealing with it on a daily basis . However, it wasn't the work that got to me. It was my work environment. It was toxic. I tried to block out these thoughts as I prepared for work. As I stared at my half-shaven face, I began to reflect on my extensive career. After 18 years, I made less money than when I started and was still in the same position. I was often passed over for promotions. My job did not value me. More importantly, I did not value me. I saw myself as a failure. As a result, people with fewer skills were chosen for important tasks. Despite showing up for work on time and always in a great mood I was unhappy. *Why did it take me 18 years to realize this?* Maybe I was too busy looking at my situation rather than listening to my heart. I sat on the edge of the bed, picked up the phone, and told them I would be coming in a little late. Damn it! I didn't even have enough courage to take a much-needed mental health day. I closed my eyes. As I sat motionless, a question popped into my mind: *Why wasn't I appreciated?* It was almost as if I was talking to myself. Wait! I *was* talking to myself. But this time I was listening. I answered myself, "*You* don't think you are enough!" That was it. I had answered my own question. I saw myself as inadequate. As a result, so did everyone else. I was living out my own self-image. People were just reflecting what I was projecting. I thought of myself as a problem, not as a solution. Now that I look back, I can see all my problems started with my self-image. How I saw myself determined every decision I ever made in my life. It finally dawned on me that I wasn't simply suffering from bad luck. I had a "seeing" problem. If I was going to change my life, I was going to have to see differently. However, it would take me years to discover seeing comes from hearing.

# Small Opportunities Lead to Big Outcomes: Answer the Call

*The boy Samuel ministered before the LORD under Eli. In those days the word of the LORD was rare; there were not many visions.*

*One night Eli, whose eyes were becoming so weak that he could barely see, was lying down in his usual place. The lamp of God had not yet gone out, and Samuel was lying down in the house of the LORD, where the ark of God was. Then the LORD called Samuel.*

*Samuel answered, "Here I am." And he ran to Eli and said, "Here I am; you called me."*

*But Eli said, "I did not call; go back and lie down." So he went and lay down.*

*Again, the LORD called, "Samuel!" And Samuel got up and went to Eli and said, "Here I am; you called me."*

*"My son," Eli said, "I did not call; go back and lie down."*

*Now Samuel did not yet know the LORD: The word of
the LORD had not yet been revealed to him.*

*A third time the LORD called, "Samuel!" And Samuel
got up and went to Eli and said, "Here I am; you called
me."*

*Then Eli realized that the LORD was calling the boy. So
Eli told Samuel, "Go and lie down, and if he calls you,
say, 'Speak, LORD, for your servant is listening.'" So,
Samuel went and lay down in his place.*

*The LORD came and stood there, calling as at the other
times, "Samuel! Samuel!"*

*Then Samuel said, "Speak, for your servant is
listening."*

*I Samuel 3:1-10 NIV*

One day, when I was still working as a
detective, the office phone rang. I stared at the
unknown number on the caller ID. I hoped
someone else in the office would answer. The
constant ringing was working on my nerves. My
ears could not take it any longer. I finally snatched
the phone from the cradle after the fourth ring.

*"Special Victims Unit, Detective McNeil, how may I direct your call?"* A male voice on the other end stated he needed a favor. *Oh boy!* I thought. I quickly searched the database in my brain where I kept all my good lies, looking for an excuse to hang up the phone. Just as I found the right lie to tell, the person interrupted. The man on the phone stated he was looking for a detective who could give a class. *Well, that counted me out,* I thought. I tried to give my wonderful lie, but the bossy, deep voice continued to explain details about the class. The class would be given to a group of sexual assault nurses on how to collect DNA for sexual assault investigations. I informed the person that no one was in the office, but I would ask around. The caller informed me it was a non-paying gig and he needed an answer soon. I knew immediately no detective in our office would take the offer. I told the caller it would be difficult trying to get a detective to work for free on their off time. The caller then asked if I might be interested. Wait! Did he not hear what I just said? NO detective would be interested in taking a non-paying job. I tried to use silence as my answer. However, the caller just waited for a response. Finally, he asked again if I would be interested. I reluctantly agreed. I later learned I had to travel nearly one hundred miles to teach the class. I

wanted to call back and decline, but I had given my word.

The day arrived for me to teach the class. I walked into the classroom and noticed a whopping six students. The tension in my muscles began to increase. Somehow, the small crowd made me more nervous. The fact I could read their facial expressions made me feel small. Each participant was giving a look of curiosity. Though they all looked eager to hear what I had to say, I must admit I felt a bit disappointed. I was under the impression I would be speaking to a classroom full of people. After calming my nerves, I began to tell my personal story of abuse. My story connected with those in the audience and I noticed some people in the audience were crying. Afterwards the questions came pouring in. *"How did you overcome your abuse?" "Did you ever tell anyone?"* Some of the attendees shared their stories of abuse with me. I was shocked. What I thought would be an embarrassing moment turned out to be a wonderful opportunity to share my story with others who cared. Until that moment I had never told anyone. I kept it a secret. Sharing my story helped me released some of the pain and guilt I had bottled inside. More importantly, it was a moment for others to release their pain. What I thought was a tedious assignment turned out to be a healing opportunity from God. That dreaded phone call in the office changed my life. God had called me. And, like Samuel, I had to be in a position to truly hear it. I almost missed my calling because I was too busy thinking about what I lacked. And, like Samuel, I was looking to other people for direction instead of listening for God's voice. Are you listening to small opportunities God has placed in front of you, or are you waiting on your big break? Instead of thinking about what you don't have, think of your life as an opportunity to bless someone else. What small opportunities do you have right now?

**Trusting God's Voice**

*Trust in the LORD with all your heart, and do not lean on your own understanding. Proverbs 3:5*

The following month I was asked to speak again. I continued to teach the class for several months. One day the instructor asked if I would be willing to travel out of town to speak. She informed me that an organization heard about me and wanted me to teach a class at their conference. However, they were only willing to pay for my hotel room; I would not get paid for speaking. The class would be at a resort in North Carolina;

nearly two-hundred miles away. I hesitated. I did not have reliable transportation to travel that far. My new 2014 BMW had just been repossessed and I was driving an old beat up 1997 Toyota Camry. The vehicle was leaking every fluid imaginable, had bald tires, and the shocks and struts needed to be replaced. My mind wanted to say, "No," but my big mouth took over and said "Yes!" I went home and wondered, *How was I going to make this happen?* I had no money and my car only had a half a tank of gas. I would be able to make it to the conference, but I wouldn't have enough gas to make it back. I could not understand why God would ask me to do something like this without resources. God was again asking me to step out on faith. Like David, I was learning an important lesson: *God always ask us to follow His voice, even when it's inconvenient.*

The day finally arrived. I grabbed a sandwich bag containing five dollars in coins which I was saving for an emergency. I jumped in my hooptie and drove up the Georgia mountains. The car sputtered and shook all the way up the mountains. I prayed throughout the whole trip. Driving up to the conference center, I passed a Bojangles restaurant with a huge marquee sign that read: *five pieces for $3.99*. I screamed for joy. I pulled into the drive-thru and apologized to the cashier for handing her a bag full of coins. She laughed. The cashier handed me my five delicious pieces of chicken. I drove to my room, ate my chicken, and went to bed.

The next morning, I arrived at my assigned classroom. The room was full of veteran law enforcement officers, social workers, and attorneys. I wondered if they would even listen to an unknown detective from Georgia. I calmed down and reminded myself that this was an assignment from God. I told my story just as I had in Georgia. The room erupted in applause. The next morning, I returned to the same classroom and noticed people standing outside the door. The organizers were bringing extra chairs into the room. Somehow word had gotten out about the class and nearly everyone signed up to attend. I was stunned. After the class, the organizers invited me to dinner. At the dinner, attendees from the conference handed me business cards and asked if I would speak at their local conferences. Of course, I agreed. I went back to my room, laid on my bed, and stared at the ceiling in disbelief.

The next day I woke up and loaded up my car. It was time to go home. As I drove down the mountain I knew God had summoned me. Little did I know that one class would lead me to the greatest opportunity of my life. The class allowed me to discover my gift for teaching. It was a small assignment, but it led to big changes. Because I begrudgingly agreed to teach a class to a small group of nurses, I was eventually able to resign and teach full time. I also met my future wife in one of those classes. One opportunity turned into a life-changing experience. To think I almost turned down the opportunity just because I would not get paid for it! Opportunities like these don't come easy, but when they show up they bring out the best in us.

# A Rocky Start

I love the movie Rocky. In it Sylvester Stallone played a small-time boxer who had big dreams. In the beginning, no one believed in him. He had a rocky start (pun intended), but he would eventually go on to become a world champion. When I discovered the true story behind the movie I fell in love with it even more. Sylvester Stallone wrote the script for the movie in three and half days after being inspired by a Muhammad Ali fight. After writing the script, he began to shop it around to movie producers. No one was interested. When someone finally made him an offer, Sylvester Stallone was told he could not star in the movie. Stallone rejected the offer and insisted he be given the starring role. He was eventually given the role and as they say, "The rest is history."

We all love a good rag-to-riches story because they allow us to have hope. The stories communicate that we too can accomplish the impossible. We watch with excitement as the underdog overcomes the odds. However, it's easy to cheer for an underdog in a movie, but not so easy when you are the underdog yourself. I found this out the hard way when I left my job.

It wasn't easy leaving my job. The job security made it difficult. Getting paid a set amount of money every two weeks was comforting. In addition, my job was predictable and came with good benefits. When I resigned, all those perks disappeared immediately. I was on my own. I didn't know anything about the public speaking business. Yet, here I was with a public speaking company and no booked clients. I wasn't even good at public speaking. I had preached in churches before, but this was different. In church people pretended to like you even if they thought you sucked. People who paid an admission to hear me speak wouldn't be as forgiving. One thing was for sure: if I was going to make it as a speaker, I had to hustle. I heard this word often but did not know what it meant. Hustling meant you not only have to look for opportunities, but you have to create them. Working a job is easy because you are given instruction and a job description. You can get by fulfilling the specific requirements. However, when you start a business everything is unpredictable. Money does not show up every two weeks. In fact, in the beginning, it might not show up at all. Initially, I had to pay to use my gift before my gift would start paying me. I wished I would have learned this lesson before quitting my job. I had to learn this lesson in the field (wilderness). It is in the field (wilderness) where you learn faith. It is here you are stripped of everything. You learn the principle of sacrifice. The principle of sacrifice says you must be willing to give up your present life to create a better life. Your real lessons in life come by what you are willing to give up. Often God will give you a chance to stay in your current position. God will force you to choose between comfort and purpose. When I resigned from my job, I was offered a huge raise to stay. I turned it down. My gift was calling me. I had to answer. In order to walk toward my gift, I had to walk away from my security. The same will be true for you. God will test you to see how bad you want to pursue your gift.

I was new on the speaking circuit and not many people were willing to pay me. I had to speak for free on many occasions to get my name out there. My friends told me I was stupid for speaking for free. I argued it was a wonderful opportunity for me. Teaching others compelled me to learn more about my abuse and how it affected other people. It also allowed me to get accustomed to standing in front of people sharing my passion. My colleagues could not recognize the opportunity, because they were blinded by money. Money by itself is not bad. It is our beliefs about money that can lead us astray. We are led to believe that money will take away all of our problems. As a result, we equate money with happiness. You will never find happiness chasing money. Someone will always have more money than you. Instead, focus on opportunities to find significance in your life. Look at your current job as an opportunity to bring change into the world. It will not only change your outlook on life but will also separate you from your peers. Instead of complaining about problems, seek opportunities. However, opportunities only reveal themselves to those who are willing to be responsible.

# Pray for Responsibility

*From everyone who has been given much, much will be demanded; and from the one who has been entrusted with much, much more will be asked.* Luke 12:48 NIV

As a minister, I listened to a lot of prayer requests. People rarely prayed for more responsibility or small opportunities. The requests comprised of desires for healing, financial freedom, love, or a million-dollar business. People often pray for complete blessings. God does not give us anything in complete form. God will often give a partial blessing and observe how we respond. God wants to see how responsible we are with what we are given. Often these partial blessings come in the form of opportunities. We are provided an opportunity and ask to be responsible.  We should change our prayer requests. Rather than asking for things, we should ask for opportunities. Why would anyone ask God for an opportunity? Because God loves giving opportunities, because they test our ability to be responsible. He gave Adam and Eve a garden. David and Moses were given sheep. Jesus was given twelve disciples. God wants to see how responsible you are with small opportunities before giving you more important tasks. As the Bible guides us, *"God is faithful; he will not let you be tempted beyond what you can bear." (1 Corinthians 10:13 NIV).* You must not only learn how to accept responsibility; you must also learn to give it. When God calls you to your purpose you will have to make tough decisions. One of those decisions will be who to take with you on your journey.

## God Doesn't Want a Lot

*Now Lot, who was moving about with Abram, also had flocks and herds and tents. But the land could not support them while they stayed together, for their possessions were so great that they were not able to stay together. And quarreling arose between Abram's herders and Lot's. The Canaanites and Perizzites were also living in the land at that time.*

*So Abram said to Lot, "Let's not have any quarreling between you and me, or between your herders and mine, for we are close relatives. ⁹ Is not the whole land before you? Let's part company. If you go to the left, I'll go to the right; if you go to the right, I'll go to the left."*

*Lot looked around and saw that the whole plain of the Jordan toward Zoar was well watered, like the garden of the LORD, like the land of Egypt. (This was before the LORD destroyed Sodom and Gomorrah.¹) So Lot chose for himself the whole plain of the Jordan and set out toward the east. The two men parted company:* ¹²*Abram lived in the land of Canaan, while Lot lived among the cities of the plain and pitched his tents near Sodom.* ¹³*Now the people of Sodom were wicked and were sinning greatly against the LORD.*

¹⁴**The LORD said to Abram after Lot had parted from him**, *"Look around from where you are, to the north and south, to the east and west.* ¹⁵*All the land that you see I will give to you and your offspring[a] forever.* ¹⁶*I will make your offspring like the dust of the earth, so that if anyone could count the dust, then your offspring could be counted.* ¹⁷*Go, walk through the length and breadth of the land, for I am giving it to you."*
Genesis 13:5-17

A year into running my business I was forced to terminate my first employee. The employee was responsible for booking all my speaking engagements. She was the first contact people had with my company. She was a wonderful person, but she was irresponsible.

Money was her motivation. She would not return phone calls or answer emails. As a result, a lot of people did not want to book me to speak, and I gained a reputation for being difficult to book. Because she simply wanted money, I was losing it. So, let me warn you: When you start walking in your purpose, stay away from people who only crave money. They will obstruct your vision. Remember when Abraham took Lot with him? Lot's desire for wealth got Abraham into all sorts of trouble. Lot obstructed Abrahams vision. Lot's name means, "to cover or to obstruct." Abraham brought Lot on the journey. As a result, he was not able to fully see God's vision for his life. The Bible says after Lot departed, God was then able to show Abraham the full vision. Remember, you want someone who is an asset, not a liability to your vision. Do you have a Lot in your life? If so, it is time to downsize and go small.

You will know a Lot when you see one. They will always want more than they give. Often, when I ask people for assistance with my work, the first question is always, "How much will I be paid?" They don't even allow me to finish telling them about the project. Their desire for money blinds them to any opportunity in front of them, including the long-term financial gain that could eventually result. I would try to help them see that these opportunities were seeds that could grow into money later. I would see blank stares looking back at me. You may have to go outside your immediate circle to find reliable help with your vision. Now I know you may be saying, "I have friends who will help." That's great, but be sure that your friends have a passion for your vision. If not, they too will be irresponsible. You will discover once you step into your purpose that your friends will dwindle. Your purpose will place you on a different path, one they may not want to travel.

Like most people, my friends equated success with money. As a result, they never took risks unless they involved an immediate payday. If you are going to be successful you must not think about money. Focus on opportunities and consider no opportunity as too small. Martin Luther King once stated, "*If a man is called to be a street sweeper, he should sweep streets even as a Michelangelo painted, or Beethoven composed music or Shakespeare wrote poetry. He should sweep streets so well that all the hosts of heaven and earth will pause to say, 'Here lived a great street sweeper who did his job well.' No work is insignificant. All labor that uplifts humanity has dignity and importance and should be undertaken with painstaking excellence.*" Each time I read that quote I get inspired. It makes me want to be my best. If we want to be successful, we must learn to be responsible with the opportunities we are given. Success does not depend on how much money you make but how well you take advantage of opportunities, which are not always obvious. It is what we do with the opportunities that determines our success. What good is having things if we are irresponsible with them? We each get 168 hours in a week. Most people waste much of this time chasing after big, obvious opportunities. As a result, they pass up small opportunities each day. People look for a big breakthrough, but breakthroughs happen to those who have prepared themselves through the opportunities they have been given. This can often mean doing jobs no one else wants to do. The next time you are offered a small opportunity, embrace it. Then ask yourself how you can make the most of the opportunity. Let's look at an example of how David took advantage of a small opportunity.

*Now Jesse said to his son David, "Take this ephah of roasted grain and these ten loaves of bread for your brothers and hurry to their camp. Take along these ten cheeses to the commander of their unit. See how your brothers are and bring back some assurance from them. I Samuel 17:17-18*

David became king by taking advantage of a small opportunity. Small opportunities often appear in the form of hard, tedious work. So, if you don't like hard work, opportunities will elude you. I encountered this truth as a new detective.

## Pebbles in my Shoes.

When I became a detective, I thought my life would get easier. I had no idea of the work and transformation that was ahead of me. I knew very little as a rookie detective. But I said yes to every assignment given to me. The veteran detectives gave me all their unwanted cases. I admit, some of these cases were difficult. I still took on these responsibilities and never complained. After a while, my hard work paid off. It wasn't long before I surpassed all the veteran detectives in the office. I won several awards and became the most sought after detective in my department. And it all started by taking unwanted opportunities. You will get opportunities, but they may come in the form of work no one else wants. Do not worry. This is a sign the opportunity is from God. God knows if an obviously amazing opportunity was presented, everyone would volunteer. So, God often conceals blessings in unwanted tasks. Moses was told to go speak to Pharaoh. Gideon was asked to fight a large army with only 300 men. Jesus was asked to die on a cross and David was asked to go bring food to people who despised him. What David could have seen as an insult, he instead turned into an opportunity. Instead of complaining, he did as he was told. His obedience led him to an opportunity God would use to promote him. Even when David arrived with food he was not welcomed by his brothers. They ridiculed him. *Take note: You will not be welcomed by everyone. People will attempt to discourage you from being different.* The unwanted tasks God gives you may not look like much in the beginning. However, these are tests. God wants to see how you handle small opportunities and opposition. I hope you caught that bit of wisdom. God will always give you *opposition with the small opportunity.* The decision to accept both will separate you. The step you take toward God will always be a step away from the norm.

# One Giant Step—The Day I Quit my Job

I packed the last of my things. I stood up from my desk and noticed a book lying on the corner of my desk. It was Steve Harvey's book, *Jump: Take the Leap of Faith to Achieve Your Life Abundance.* I picked it up and placed it in my bag, chuckling. Never in a million years did I think I would be leaving a secure job to start my own business. It was a bittersweet moment for me. It wasn't at all how I envisioned it. There was no big announcement or email sent through the department. No one stood outside my cubicle telling me how much they would miss me and crying. I second-guessed my decision. No one thought it was a clever idea, including me. No one showing up for my departure seemed to be a sign I was making a mistake. When other people left the department, it was a big deal. They were given huge parties and fancy plaques. I was leaving, and not even my desk seemed disappointed. One thing I knew for sure was that I could no longer stay where my spirit felt so depleted. I was doing great work, but it didn't seem to be having an impact. For every abuse case I closed, I would be assigned three more. The job was stressing me out and my health was declining as a result. As I walked out of the building for the last time, I briefly looked over my shoulders. It would be my final day as a detective. After 20 years of serving my community and protecting children from predators, I decided to walk away. As I walked, I reflected on a question posed by a fellow detective, "Are you feeling emotional?" My answer was, "No! Of course not." At least, I was not feeling sad. Maybe I should have been emotional. After all, I was walking away from a secure job with no money in my bank account. My mortgage was coming due, and I wasn't sure if I would have the money. In addition to that, I had no health insurance. So, yes, I should have been feeling sorry for myself, but I was instead feeling excited. I was feeling sad for the people I was leaving behind. I knew most of them felt trapped and were not happy. They thought I had this tremendous courage and took a big leap of faith. However, the truth is, I did not take a giant leap. I took small steps that allowed me to make this big leap.

I exited the building. As I got into my Uber, a small tear formed in the corner of my eye. I had just taken the biggest jump of my life. Now I was wondering if my parachute would open like Steve Harvey promised in his book, or if I would crash and die.

Months went by, and my new business was blossoming. I was speaking across the country, but I had yet to receive any type of payment. I was surviving on credit cards. I started to worry. One day I got an unexpected surprise when I checked my mailbox. As the key turned and the metal door opened, my heart raced with anticipation. My eyes peered into the tiny box, and that is when I saw the beautiful phrase that read, *Pay to the Order of Kevin McNeil*. My eyes grew big and a smile grew wide on my face. It was a check. I signed it and prepared to take it to the bank the next day. Things were finally looking up.

The next day, I got dressed and headed out the door to deposit my check. As I drove, I began to think about the conversations I'd had with several Child Advocacy Center directors about the difficulty of raising money. Child Advocacy Centers are where abused children and their families go to get help and heal. As I was traveling the country speaking, I was learning a horrible truth: One of our nation's most valuable resources was not well funded. In my many years as a detective, I watched our local Child Advocacy

Center give children and families hope. Knowing this, I felt bad as I pulled up to the bank. I was about to cash a check written to me by a Child Advocacy Center for speaking at their conference. I tried to reason with myself that I deserved it. My heart told me the children deserved it more. I thought about my bills and ignored my heart. I went into the bank and deposited the check. I drove home, feeling ill at ease. As I pulled into my subdivision, I saw a family walking in the neighborhood. They reminded me of the many families I saw come to the Child Advocacy Center for help. I went inside, pulled out my checkbook and made a check out to a Child Advocacy Center in the same amount I had just received. It was the largest donation of any kind I had ever given. Now I was back at square one, with no money. Little did I know; this small decision would have a profound                                    impact.

# Find Your Fight

*David said to Saul, "Let no one lose heart on account of this Philistine; your servant will go and fight him."*

*Saul replied," You are not able to go out against this Philistine and fight him; you are only a young man, and he has been a warrior from his youth."*
I Samuel 17:32-33

I sat in the front row of the church pews waiting to speak. I was nervous and my palms were sweating. The two speakers before me had doctorate degrees. They discussed profound, theological concepts. I heard things about the Bible I had never even considered. I was in awe of their knowledge and the revelation being taught. I almost forgot I was there as a speaker myself. I had been invited to the church conference to speak about protecting children from abuse. When the two speakers were done, we took a fifteen-minute break. After the break, it was my turn to speak. The pastor introduced me as a special victims' detective with years of experience investigating abuse crimes. The church grew silent. I rose from my seat and nervously approached the pulpit of the church. My eyes looked out at the attentive crowd. I could sense that the topic made them understandably uneasy. I rushed through my presentation, made my closing remarks, and took my seat. Afterward, the pastor invited all of the speakers on stage to answer any questions from the audience. I was not prepared to answer any questions, and I expected they would not have many for me anyway. I was surprised when one person after another stood up and directed their questions at me. It appeared I had struck a chord in the church. One woman in particular stood with tears flowing down her face. She was trembling so badly two people had to help her stand. She was a petite woman, who appeared to be in her late forties. I didn't know what she would say, and she blurted out, *"Thank you! You have finally answered so many questions for me."* She began to say she was a victim of childhood abuse and my presentation explained some of her erratic behavior. The woman said she blamed herself and asked God for healing. She stated she had attended church all her life, but no one was ever able to explain her pain in the way I had just done. Tears began to build in my eyes. I was at a loss for words. The woman continued to speak of her addiction to sex and drugs because of her abuse. As the woman spoke,

I saw two ushers quickly get up and escort her out the sanctuary. The pastor stated they wanted to "deal with her" in private. I never got a chance to respond to her, but I noticed several people in the audience crying. I wondered how many other people in the audience had similar pasts. Questions flooded my mind. How were people able to attend church every Sunday yet not be healed from their childhood trauma? How did carrying this baggage affect their worshipping experience and their life?

On my long drive home, I pondered this question. I thought about my own healing journey. I remember how afraid I was to talk about the pain from my abuse. I kept it all bottled up inside. Like the lady who resonated with me, I attended church for years but thought God could not hear my pain. The truth was, I was not all the way healed, but at least I was on a healing journey. I had survived for years with an injured heart. Like the woman, sex and alcohol became my way of coping. Speaking at the church made me realize my purpose was not just to help people understand abuse; it was to help them heal from it. Abuse was the enemy I was born to fight. I knew I had found my purpose, because like David I had to fight for it. I had come face to face with my Goliath. I was up on that stage not to teach, but to start a fight with an enemy destroying God's creation. What about you - what has God called you to fight? Find your fight and you will discover the path to your purpose.

My experience at the church conference helped me focus. I had to do more to educate people on the effects of abuse. I made the decision to dedicate the remainder of my days on Earth fighting abuse and raising awareness of its effects.

.

# Never Despise Small Beginnings

*"Then he took his staff in his hand and chose five smooth stones from the brook and put them in his shepherd's pouch. His sling was in his hand, and he approached the Philistine."*

1 Samuel 17:40

Several weeks passed. I was able to pay my bills, but I was barely surviving. Money was tight. My friends had stopped calling and hanging out with me. I no longer had a vehicle and was too often stuck in the house, bored. I was unhappy and depressed. I had taken a leap of faith and saw no results so far. I began to question my decision. Worst-case scenarios flooded my mind. Thoughts of sleeping under a bridge kept me up many nights. I considered moving back home with my mother, but my two brothers were already living there. My presence would have been a burden. But my worst fears were returning and I entertained the idea of begging for my old job back. I imagined all the people who would greet me with, "I told you so!" One night, I sat on my couch with my head in my hands. My normal way of dealing with disappointment was to grab my favorite alcoholic beverage and drink myself to sleep. However, I grew up watching my stepfather drink himself to death because of depression and I fought back that urge.

I needed some inspiration, so I picked up my Bible and began to read. I read the story of Moses and how God used him to deliver a nation from bondage. I noticed God did not give Moses a large army, nor did he give him great physical ability. He gave Moses a word and a rod. That seemed odd to me. I thought, *God, you want a known fugitive to go tell an Egyptian King to free slaves, and all you give him is a word and a rod. Yeah, right! The least you could have done was tell the Pharaoh that Moses was coming and that you sent him.* God also did not do much to ensure Moses would be successful. Moses had to go with little evidence that God was with him. Yet, he took what God gave him and marched right into Pharaoh's palace unafraid. Moses knew that to appear before a king without being summoned could potentially result in death. And still, he went anyway. Moses' bravery was based on his complete trust in God. The story taught me a lesson when it came to trusting God. God will often place you in a life and death situation with little evidence He is with you. It takes bravery to follow God. You will not be given any sign or promise – you may not have your own burning bush. God will give you very little and see what you do with what you have.

After reading this, I realized I had done the same thing when I resigned from my job. I didn't have much evidence that it was the smart decision. Most importantly, my heart was set on impacting the world in a positive way. After serving my country as a solider and my community as a police officer, I wanted to do even more. I asked myself what I had at my disposal that I could utilize. What was my small stone? What was my rod? My mind went back to my childhood, when I used to send money to starving kids in faraway countries. As far back as I could remember, I wanted to help children in need. In fact, I had subconsciously chosen a job as a detective protecting such children. Now I was out in the world with no connection to children for the first time in my life. My desire was to find a way to continue to help children heal from the effects of abuse. I figured the best way to do that was to write a book, even though the idea seemed absolutely crazy.

None of my friends were authors. I decided to share my intention with a few friends. I told them I was going to write a children's book about overcoming abuse. They didn't laugh, but they didn't exactly encourage me, either. I decided to write the book despite not having the money or encouragement. It took me about three months to finish. I intentionally made the book small, so it could be read in one sitting. . Getting the book published was not easy. Due to lack of money, I had to self-publish the book. No publisher wanted to invest in an unknown author. I was hopeful people I knew would support me. I was extremely excited when I finally released the hardcopy version of my book on Amazon. I encouraged my family and friends to purchase a copy and spread the word. I flooded every social media platform I could find. Six months went by, and I'd sold a whopping six copies. It seemed my effort to become an author had failed. I wanted to give up, but I refused. I was convinced I just needed to get the book into the right hands, people who wanted to be healed. If I couldn't sell the book, I would do the next best thing.

I decided to give my book away. I was convinced it contained valuable information that would help people get free from their internal struggles and pain. At first, I was receiving no feedback from readers, even those to whom I gave a free copy. I didn't know if the book was resonating with readers or insulting them. Eventually, as time passed, I slowly started getting text messages saying, "OMG your book had me in tears," or "Your book is so powerful." It was then I discovered the problem. People were not reading my book. When the book arrived in the mail, people just laid it aside. Because the book was small, some people assumed it had no value. However, those who did read it, reported they benefited from its message. I was angry at first, but I realized we all make this mistake: We take small things for granted. I, too, was guilty of this mistake. The experience taught me a valuable lesson. Don't despise small beginnings. Small things matter to God. In fact, I would continue to learn that *small* was how God did business.

KEVIN McNEIL

# Close Your Eyes and Listen

*Look Mom! I'm in Hollywood!*

I was excited. I couldn't wait to step off the plane. I was finally visiting a place I had only seen on television. I was going to Hollywood, and I let all my friends know it. I couldn't wait to take pictures and post them to Facebook, Instagram, and Twitter. I looked forward to seeing their responses. As I sat on the plane, I thought about all the tourist attractions. My excitement grew as the pilot announced we were making our final descent into Los Angeles. As we landed and taxied toward the gate, I wondered if I would see any celebrities just casually walking through the airport.

Once off the plane, I wandered the airport with camera in hand. My eyes darted back and forth, looking at every face walking in my direction. As I made my way through LAX, I saw no celebrities. Disappointed, I made my way to get my bags and requested an Uber. When he arrived, I got into the car and wondered if perhaps celebrities entered the airport at a different terminal. Maybe there was a VIP entrance. I was a little disappointed by the lack of sightings as we made our way to the W Hotel in the center of Hollywood. When I arrived, I noticed Bentleys and Mercedes parked at the entrance. I tried to imagine who could possibly own these incredibly expensive vehicles. The ambiance confirmed that I was at the happening spot in the city. There were large groups of scantily dressed people walking in and out of the lobby. Security was everywhere. You would have thought the President was arriving soon. I immediately felt out of place. I wondered if my workout sweats and faded T-shirt were even appropriate. I clearly didn't look like I belonged, but I wasn't too concerned with my appearance. Besides, I was in Los Angeles to speak at a celebrity fundraiser. However, I would soon discover that not only is image important in Hollywood, it is *everything*.

I gathered my belongings as the hotel personnel rushed over to open my passenger door. The hotel was amazing. I couldn't t believe that I was able to have a room in such a beautiful building. Thankfully, I didn't have to worry about the cost of the room, which was paid for by the organization that flew me out to speak. It was such an exciting time for me. I felt like all my arduous work was finally beginning to pay off. I smiled at the doorman as I walked through the grand entrance doors. The hotel had several bars and restaurants. I walked up to reception, and the young lady looked at me and asked if I needed help, or if I was looking for somewhere in particular. I thought it was obvious I was there to get a room. Although I had a large suitcase and a large backpack, she did not see me as a plausible guest. I informed her I was there to check into the hotel. She paused and asked, "Check in here? What is your name?" I told her. She repeated my name just to make sure. "Kevin McNeil?" She told me the computer showed I was staying for two nights in one of their most luxurious rooms. As I waited for her to hand me my hotel key, I noticed a concerned look come over her face. She asked me if I had the credit card that paid for the room. I explained to her I was in town to speak at an event and the room was booked for me. She told me that because it was such an expensive room, I would have to produce the actual credit card that was used to book it. She told me I needed to prove that the room was reserved for me. I told her I did not have the card. The room was paid for and booked in my name. She asked me if I had a credit card. I told her I had several. She told me what she could do, was refund the money back to the person's card who paid for the room and charge my card for the amount owed on the room. I thought that sounded ridiculous. Why would you charge me for a room that was already paid for? The lady said she could not let me check in unless I was willing to pay for the room with my personal credit card. I didn't understand. The room was already paid for in full. I then noticed what was happening: I simply didn't fit. She saw me as a small person in a big world. I did not fit the agent's assumed image of someone who could afford such an expensive room. I asked myself, "Was this racism or something else?" I think it was a little bit of both. I came to Hollywood with the feeling I was finally on the verge of making it big. Now I wasn't so sure. One thing I did know for sure was that I felt incredibly small.

As I waited in the lobby to get my room key, I felt so embarrassed. I had to call the person who had reserved the room and ask her to speak with the manager before the room could be approved. After waiting for nearly an hour, I was finally given my key. I hurried to my room, changed into my suit, stored my bags, and headed downstairs to await my ride. The suit made me more comfortable and helped me to look the part, but I still felt like a small fish in a large pond. If I felt like this already, how would I feel when I arrived at the fundraiser? Although I had not seen any celebrities at the airport, I was certain to meet several at the fundraiser. These thoughts left me already feeling inadequate. My ride arrived, and I got into the vehicle and was whisked away to one of Hollywood's most prestigious neighborhoods. I was greeted by the host as I exited the vehicle. Thoughts flooded my mind. I hoped I would fit in. I hoped I would feel comfortable. And most importantly, I hoped I would not make a fool of myself.

As I entered the magnificent residence, I was introduced to the homeowners. They were the nicest people in the world. I immediately felt at home. It was significantly different from my experience at the hotel.

I made myself comfortable and introduced myself to the guests who had arrived previously. After about a half hour, more guests started to arrive. I noticed a lot of familiar faces from television and magazine covers. After conversing with the guests for a while, it was time for me to speak. The host introduced me. I walked up to the platform. I could see all the beautiful faces present. The people were really engaged and awaiting what I had to say. As I spoke, I could see their hearts were cheering for me to succeed. My nervousness melted away. I was worried how people from Hollywood would view me, a small-town boy from Memphis, Tennessee. But it seemed I was worried about the wrong thing. The people saw me as one of them. I was the one concerned with image, not the people in the audience. I had it all wrong. Television made me believe successful people saw themselves as "better than." They didn't see themselves as better, but they did view themselves as valuable members of the world. All this time I was projecting my insecurities upon people. The truth is, we all do this to some extent. We produce images in our heads. Often the images are not of other people, but of ourselves. We see other people as giants because of our distorted self-image.

After I spoke, the people were so kind, grateful, and generous. They all told me they were glad I had agreed to travel such a great distance and speak at their event. I was there both to speak and to help raise money for child abuse awareness and education. It was a subject many people did not typically want to discuss. However, the people in attendance were genuinely interested in what I had to say. I mingled with the crowd and had great conversations that were authentic and engaging. All the people I spoke with shared their ideas for making the world a better place. They talked about their children and how they wanted to leave the world improved for them. I was stunned. I'd imagined I would be engrossed with stories of success and how much money they made.

While I was concerned about my image, I noticed the wealthy guests were clearly focused on making the world better. They were not image-seekers. In fact, many of them weren't concerned with their image at all. I'd had it all wrong. Hollywood wasn't full of rich people concerned about their representation. The people I met were more concerned with making an impact on the world. It was people like me and the people gathered outside the W Hotel that were concerned about image. We were the ones standing in lines to buy expensive tennis shoes and overpriced gadgets, our minds focused on making it big – or at least making it seem like we've made it big. Meanwhile, the people with all the power made a living by using small things to make an enormous impact. I realized again that if I wanted to solve big problems, I would have to start small. But before I began, I needed to have my eyes checked. I was using my eyes to see and not to listen. My hotel experience was a result of what I was telling myself. I was communicating I did not belong; it wasn't the clerk. She was just listening.

KEVIN McNEIL

.

# The Problem with Seeing

*For the world offers only a craving for physical pleasure, a craving for everything we see, and pride in our achievements and possessions. These are not from the Father but are from this world. 1 John 2:16 NLT*

As a police officer, I frequently entered people's homes. As part of my safety routine, I had to pay attention to everything. One mistake could cost me my life in an instant. While I would look for obvious dangers, like a gun or knife, I wasn't paying attention to other things. Still, I did notice something that was common in almost every home I visited. It didn't matter if I was in the most impoverished neighborhood in the city, everyone seemed to have a nice television. Often, they had more than one. I never thought much of this until I was assigned to work in more affluent areas. Some of the homes in the affluent neighborhoods had televisions, but not as many as people living in impoverished communities. Again, I didn't give this much thought until many years later, when I found myself talking to some of the most powerful, influential people in America. As I walked into their homes, I noticed there were rarely televisions at all. I wondered, *"Why do unsuccessful people own more televisions than those who are successful?"* Then it dawned on me. People with big dreams love to watch television and fantasize about success. These were the people who could tell you about every reality show. They could name all the characters on *The Real Housewives of Atlanta*. These people loved to be entertained. But why? The answer came to me when I started getting serious about my own success. When I was dreaming of success, I loved driving in neighborhoods with million-dollar homes. I marveled at pastors who had large churches and flew on private jets. I admired sports stars, with their fancy suits and signature shoes. I also watched a lot of television. However, when I got serious about making an impact in the world, TV was the first thing to go. I no longer sat in my living room watching CNN and complaining about how bad the world had become. I wasn't concerned with the next episode of *Empire* or *Power*. I was too busy planning out and executing my own life's work. When I took my eyes off the television, I was able to see more clearly. I discovered that eyes are good for watching, but it takes vision to impact the world.

I heard people talk about "vision" all the time. It had become a buzz word, much like the word "purpose." After hearing it so often I began to drown it out my consciousness. The brain learns to ignore things after they show no importance to an individual. So, like most people, I gave vision no thought. It wasn't until I started going to leadership conferences and spending time with successful people that I understood this concept. People with vision saw things others didn't. They were solution-focused. More importantly, when I started having conversations with them, they never talked much about problems. Instead, they talked about their vision for a better world – their solutions. They were more concerned about the impact than they were about making money. Initially I thought like most people: *Of course, they were not worried about problems, they had none. Anyone can focus on saving the world when they have no big worries like mortgages, food on the table, getting into college, or keeping the lights on.* However, I soon discovered they were not successful because they had large sums of money. The people I encountered were successful because they used small solutions to solve a big problem. Like most people, I had it backwards. I was looking for a big solution to my big problems. I had been ignoring the truly important things. The story of David and Goliath teaches us that God uses people who can see what others cannot. David's gift wasn't his strength; it was his vision. But before you get stuck on vision I must warn you vision has nothing to do with the eyes. Vision comes from hearing, not seeing.

*"So, then faith comes by hearing, and hearing by the word of God."* Romans 10:17 KJV

Our vision is controlled by how we hear ourselves. Saul and Israel saw a giant because they listened to their fear. David saw an opportunity to honor God. David didn't listen to fear, but rather God's promises. David's vision allowed him to see beyond the problem and hear God's instruction. If you want to be successful, you must ask God to give you vision. Vision is the ability to hear God's voice. Wow! Did you hear that? Vision is **not** about seeing. It is about hearing. You are a listening spirit. Your whole life is based on what you hear, not what you see. Your life is a result of what or who you have been listening to most of your life.

Your thoughts are sound waves that literally shape how you see the world. Your sight is determined by what you think. Your brain wires itself to your thoughts (as a man thinks; *Proverbs 23:7*) and directs your attention to what you think about the most. If you always have negative thoughts, you will then be attracted to negative things; in turn negative things will be attracted to you. Wow! I hope you caught that revelation. Much like God, you are creating your world with thoughts.

Pause right now and ask yourself, *"How do I hear myself?"* Wait! Don't answer. Listen! If you did it correctly you should have heard your spirit answer. You must learn to hear your spirit. When God speaks, He speaks to your spirit. If you do not silence the negative voices in your spirit, you will have a tough time hearing God's voice. God is always speaking, but you must be on the same frequency to hear what God is saying to you.

Allow me to give you an example on how this works. Turn on your radio. Tune it to a station you like. Now, turn off the radio. What happened to the sound? Most people will say the sound stopped when the radio turned off. The sound never stopped, the receiver just stopped listening. Now turn back on the radio. What happened? The receiver was turned on, not the sound. Okay, leave the radio on. This time change the frequency.

What happened to your favorite music? Did it stop playing? No! You started listening to another frequency. You can't listen to two stations with one receiver. The same is true for your inner self.

You cannot listen to both God and man concurrently. You are a receiver (listening spirit) who can tune in to its own frequency. This is why the Bible instructs, *"We demolish arguments and every pretension that sets itself up against the knowledge of God, and we take captive every thought to make it obedient to Christ" (2 Corinthians 10:5)* You must pay attention to what frequency you are listening to. Success will elude you if you keep telling yourself you are inadequate. God voice is always on a positive frequency. If you are tuned in to the wrong frequency, you will not hear God. In fact, God must compete with the voices in your life before He can speak to you.

Your voice is powerful because you trust it. Your voice is familiar to you. Your eyes focus on what you tell yourself. For instance, if I tell myself I want a Porsche 911, I will begin to see them everywhere. More Porsche vehicles didn't just appear out of thin air But my voice called them to my attention. (By the way, I don't want a Porsche 911. I want a new Lincoln Navigator. My voice said my life would get better if I had one.) What is your voice telling you? You must gain control over your voice. Do not let other voices take up residence in your mind. If you do, they will shape how you view the world and God. Your life has been obeying your voice. It is no coincidence that the Bible starts off with God speaking things into existence. It's an example of the most powerful tool God gave us: our voices. Once our voices are silenced or distorted we become slaves to other voices.

# Adam and Eve voices got them in trouble

*When the woman saw that the fruit of the tree was good for food and pleasing to the eye, and also desirable for gaining wisdom, she took some and ate it. She also gave some to her husband, who was with her, and he ate it. 7 Then the eyes of both of them were opened, and they realized they were naked; so they sewed fig leaves together and made coverings for themselves. Genesis 3:6-7*

Notice it was how they spoke to themselves that finally changed how they saw themselves. This is what is meant by, "then the eyes of both of them were opened." Again, I want to emphasize that vision comes from hearing. You must not change your circumstances. You must change how you hear. In fact, you are talking to yourself now. Stop and take a listen! What did you say? Did you say something like; *"Wait I don't agree with this Kevin?"* Of course, you did because I heard you. You never stop talking. Your thoughts are invisible words. You should take some time out of your busy schedule and listen. Some people refer to this practice as meditation. Meditation is not magical.

What makes meditation so powerful is that it

allows you to hear your thoughts. Once you hear your negative thoughts you can direct them in a more positive direction. Now that you know the meaning of vision you must practice listening to it on a daily basis. Once you hear your vision, you must then repeat it as much as possible. The more you hear it, the more you will have faith in what you hear. However, I must warn you: your vision will have to compete with the other voices in your head.

Once you have vision, you will view your life differently. Your job is no longer just a place where you work. It becomes a place where God works through you. Problems now become opportunities. Failure now becomes a way to grow. God only provides vision to those who desire to honor Him in their work. Notice I said, "in their work" and not "with their mouths." Your work in the earth is your voice. What people say with their mouths is nothing but noise. A lot of people say they love God with their mouths, but do very little with their hands. Many successful people are not very religious, meaning they don't talk about God all the time. However, they do use their God-given talents to provide opportunities for other people.

They create a space for God to bless others. How do you know if you have vision? Well, ask yourself the following question: Is your goal in life to make money or to honor God?

People who see with their eyes use measurement as a guide and tool. They are the ones who ask if the cup is half empty or if it is half full. People with vision ask how they can increase the size of the cup. Visionaries don't look for problems; they solve them. David was a visionary.

Whereas Saul and his men saw Goliath's size as a problem, David viewed fighting Goliath as an opportunity to display God's power. David saw himself through God's eyes. He knew if God saw him as special, then it did not matter what mere men thought of him. David had vision (ability to hear God). Vision is when we see what God places inside of us. Instead of looking outward, we look inward. Before you continue reading, this is the first thing you will have to acknowledge: how you see (hear) yourself will determine the course of your life. God has placed everything we need in our hearts. However, when we lose sight of who we are, our eyes become our guides instead of our hearts.

# Why Is Vision so Important?

*Leave them; they are blind guides. If the blind lead the blind, both will fall into a pit.*
Matthew 15:4 NIV

You may be wondering why I would start off an inspirational book talking so much about vision. In order to answer that, I want you to close your eyes. Now, with your eyes still closed continue to read. Okay, that was a bit extreme. It is difficult to read a book with your eyes closed (unless you read braille). But my point is that you can't do much of anything with your eyes closed, except maybe sleep. Life is the same way when it comes to your spiritual eyesight. Remember that your spiritual eyesight comes from your thoughts. Your spiritual eyesight determines the direction of your life. When you do not have a vision you are living life blindly. You cannot navigate life successfully without a vision. Eyesight directs you to desires, while vision navigates you toward your purpose. A person with no vision can see the present but will have a hard time envisioning the future. The present is the only thing that matters to a person with eyesight. They are not concerned about consequences. Again, remember what happened to Adam and Eve in the Bible:

> *When the woman saw that the fruit of the tree was good for food and pleasing to the eye, and also desirable for gaining wisdom, she took some and ate it. She also gave some to her husband, who was with her, and he ate it. Then the eyes of both of them were opened, and they realized they were naked; so they sewed fig leaves together and made coverings for themselves.*
> Genesis 3:6-7 NIV

You see what happened? They were so focused what was in front of them that they did not stop to consider how their actions would impact their future. You exist in the present, but the quality of your life is determined by your future. The eyes will destroy your future. They will cause you to make rash decisions. I know this personally. When I was a young kid in the military, I spent money frivolously. It was my first time away from home and being alone. I had very little responsibility, and I made poor choices.

The military provided me with free housing, food, clothing, and healthcare. When I got paid, I had no bills. Still, I managed to create my own debt. My eyes led me on a journey to financial destruction. I did not save. I spent my money on whatever my eyes saw fit, living in the moment. Why? I had no vision for my life, so I had nowhere to direct my money, time, or energy. I listened to the negative voices in my head. I was on the wrong frequency. I was not only wasting my money; without a vision, I was wasting my life. I bought things to silence my inner voice which told me I was not enough.

What about you? How do you see (hear) your future? Are your looking (listening) at your current situation and wondering if you will ever be a success? If you are thinking like this, it means you are using your physical eyes to see what can only be seen with simple eyesight. The eyes can only focus on what's obvious and right in front of you. It takes vision to see into the future. The eyes focus on problems and are often blind to solutions. People who see only with their eyes become consumers. It takes vision to plant and invest in something you cannot yet see.

Have you ever noticed that people with the biggest problems act as if they don't see them? They blame everyone but themselves for their problems, drowning out the real problem. Let's face it, no one likes problems. We avoid them at all costs. We often pay attention to problems only when they become obvious (loud and clear) and impossible to avoid. It is then that we panic and start looking for immediate solutions. We often forget what led to the problem. You don't just become overweight; it was the extra slices of pizza and the lying on the couch. You don't all of a sudden end up in debt and file bankruptcy; it was living above your means for the last twenty years. Your marriage didn't suddenly end; it was you hanging out with the boys every weekend. In fact, very few things suddenly "happen" in our lives. If we are honest with ourselves, everything starts off small, whether good or bad. The things become storms in our lives. We stop listening and focus on the storms. Don't look at the storms; listen for God's voice. Your eyes will drown out God's voice. I want to pause and give you a very important nugget. If you get nothing else from this book, I want you to remember this: **God will never use your eyes to speak to you, nor will God use your strength to bless you.** Why? Because the eyes are limited to what they see, and the flesh is limited to its own strength. Spirit has no limitations. (*Watch and pray so that you will not fall into temptation. The spirit is willing, but the flesh is weak; Matthew 26:41*). If you want to see God in your life, you must ignore what you see and don't depend on your strength. David knew this well.

KEVIN McNEIL

# Small Nuggets to Deal with Life's Giants

*"While they may seem small, the ripple effects of small things are extraordinary."* Matt Bevin

*"Whoever can be trusted with very little can also be trusted with much, and whoever is dishonest with very little will also be dishonest with much."* Luke 16:10 NIV

The remainder of this book is designed to teach you how to notice and honor the small things in life. Small things matter, especially to God. God honors those who are faithful with little things. Learning this truth changed my life. Within two years of learning and applying this principle, I was able to resign from my job and start a successful speaking career. After twenty years of feeling stuck, I was finally free. It was not because I did anything big; rather, it was because I started honoring the small things in my life; the things I took for granted, like time, money management, and gratitude became the focus of my day. I began using my time wisely. I ceased having conversations with negative people who were not contributing to the improvement of the world. The evening news was no longer the highlight of my day. My time spent on social media decreased. I decided to walk for thirty minutes a day and spend at least fifteen minutes meditating (listening and controlling my thoughts). Within weeks, I had lost five pounds, read multiples books, created a blog, and had more energy than ever before. I was surprised how these seemingly small things made such a big impact.

This book is about how to recognize and utilize those small steps so that it will not take you twenty years to step into your destiny. I will use the story of David from the Bible as an example of how God uses small steps full of challenges to promote someone. We must remember that David did not defeat Goliath with some massive sword or shield. David defeated Goliath with a small stone. Think about that for a moment: a small man with a small stone defeated a heavily armored giant. Many people are waiting for their big break or some massive breakthrough, but I am here to tell you that the most powerful things come from the smallest resources.

Many people get discouraged because they

don't see big, immediate changes in their lives. However, I am here to tell you that God will use small things to bless you in a big way. The story of David becoming king is a perfect example. By the time David fought Goliath, he had mastered all of the small things. Instead of a sword, David used a small stone to gain victory over a giant obstacle. Don't miss that point! David used the resource God made available to him, regardless of how hopeless it might have seemed. Sure, he could have tried to use man's conventional weapons. But David didn't rely on his strength. He knew God could do big things with what seemed insignificant. God just needed someone with a big heart. The small stone in the David story represents the seed God planted inside of you, which is called "purpose." And if you pick it up, like David, and use it, you will be able to defeat any giant that gets in your path. Before God can bring you center stage to defeat your Goliath, you must prove trustworthy in the little things. David was given sheep to protect before he was given a nation to lead. He knew God often utilizes what we ignore.

This book is about how to use small steps to make big changes in life. I intentionally made the book small, because I knew many small-minded people would not read it. However, I committed to placing some of the biggest ideas God put in my heart into the book. I wanted the size of the book itself to be a message. When it comes to God, small is BIG! I want to show you how God has already armed you with what you need to conquer all your challenges. God planted a small seed inside of you called purpose. If you cultivate it, you will eventually see big blessings coming your way. Everything in life starts with a seed. Think of something right now going on in your life that is a big issue. Now think back to how the issue became big. Was there something small you ignored? If so, take out a piece of paper and write it down. It will get you in the habit of paying attention to small things.

## Every Journey Begins with One Small Step

Although we read about David's journey in a few chapters in the bible, it was a long journey before he became king. Along the way, he did not give up. He continued to take small steps forward toward fulfilling his purpose. The purposeful journey requires our willingness to take significant risks. We have to be comfortable walking into the unknown. It is here that many people fail. We want to know what the future holds and how to best prepare for it. As a result, we wait for a sign: a sign God never provides. We want our own personal Samuel to explain to us exactly what God want us to do. Your birth is a sign you are anointed (stop for a praise break). Stop waiting for proof. David was anointed king, and that was all the proof he needed to step out in faith. However, prior to being anointed, David trusted God. He trusted that wherever God led him, he would be successful. David's faith allowed him to accomplish whatever mission God assigned to him. Often, we say we trust God but we are afraid to move forward unless we are sure it is safe. This not only shows God that we don't actually trust Him, but it also shows that we don't have faith in the gifts and talents He planted inside of us. Your purpose will require you to take a step of faith into the unknown. This will require you to let go of what you are comfortable and familiar with in your life. I know this is scary. I experienced it myself. When I took the small step and decided that I was going to trust God, I nearly had a panic attack. Everything I knew and held dear to me was taken away. I lost my car. My friends dwindled. My dating life was non-existent. No woman wanted to date a man who couldn't even afford a car . I spent a lot of time alone reflecting on my life. God was dealing with my heart. Of all the things I lost and had to let go of, none was harder than letting go of my belief system.

My beliefs were hindering my faith in myself. I believed I was flawed and that something was wrong with me. My mind constantly wondered, "Why would God want someone as messed up as me?" Yet, here God was, calling me to do something great on Earth. I could not believe God would call me when I was at my lowest. I was always taught that I had to be holy and perfect before God would come anywhere near me. After reading David's story in the Bible, I changed this belief. I no longer had an excuse to sit back and wait. I saw how God used small people to do big things. All I had to do was be like David and to trust in God completely. Although this sounds simple, it was the hardest thing I ever did. It seemed like a small decision, but it had an enormous        impact        on        my        life.

# A Matter of Principle

*What David said was overheard and reported to Saul, and Saul sent for him.*

*David said to Saul, "Let no one lose heart on account of this Philistine; your servant will go and fight him."[3] Saul replied, "You are not able to go out against this Philistine and fight him; you are only a young man, and he has been a warrior from his youth."*

*But David said to Saul, "Your servant has been keeping his father's sheep. When a lion or a bear came and carried off a sheep from the flock, I went after it, struck it and rescued the sheep from its mouth. When it turned on me, I seized it by its hair, struck it and killed it.[36] Your servant has killed both the lion and the bear; this uncircumcised Philistine will be like one of them, because he has defied the armies of the living God. [37] The LORD who rescued me from the paw of the lion and the paw of the bear will rescue me from the hand of this Philistine."*

*Saul said to David, "Go, and the LORD be with you."*

*Then Saul dressed David in his own tunic. He put a coat of armor on him and a bronze helmet on his head. David fastened on his sword over the tunic and tried walking around, because he was not used to them.*

*"I cannot go in these," he said to Saul, "because I am not used to them." So he took them off. Then he took his staff in his hand, chose five smooth stones from the stream, put them in the pouch of his shepherd's bag and, with his sling in his hand, approached the Philistine.*

*Meanwhile, the Philistine, with his shield bearer in front of him, kept coming closer to David. He looked David over and saw that he was little more than a boy, glowing with health and handsome, and he despised him. He said to David, "Am I a dog, that you come at me with sticks?" And the Philistine cursed David by his gods. ⁴⁴ "Come here," he said, "and I'll give your flesh to the birds and the wild animals!"*

*David said to the Philistine, "You come against me with sword and spear and javelin, but I come against you in the name of the LORD Almighty, the God of the armies of Israel, whom you have defied. This day the LORD will deliver you into my hands, and I'll strike you down and cut off your* *head. This very day I will give the carcasses of the Philistine army to the birds and the wild animals, and the whole world will know that there is a God in Israel. <sup>47</sup> All those gathered here will know that it is not by sword or spear that the LORD saves; for the battle is the LORD's, and he will give all of you into our hands."*

*As the Philistine moved closer to attack him, David ran quickly toward the battle line to meet him. Reaching into his bag and taking out a stone, he slung it and struck the Philistine on the forehead. The stone sank into his forehead, and he fell face down on the ground.*

*So David triumphed over the Philistine with a sling and a stone; without a sword in his hand he struck down the Philistine and killed him.* 1 Samuel 17:31-50 NIV

I loved listening to my childhood pastor, Rev. Peppers, tell stories from the Bible. He would make the verses come alive and have us on the edge of our seats. My young imagination would wander off in the middle of his sermons. I would often imagine I was an Israelite soldier fighting alongside Joshua or a soldier in David's army. My favorite was when Rev. Peppers preached about

King David. I was always excited to hear how God used David to defeat this giant named Goliath. I loved how the Bible described David, a hero, as a small person. Because I was small, it inspired me when I heard God used someone like me to defeat a giant. We would play games after church and I would pretend I was King David defending God's people. As an adult, the story remains my favorite. So, it wasn't surprising I would be led to preach it many times myself. I knew the story well but missed the principle it taught. I knew God used a shepherd to fight a giant warrior. Yes, I knew it was with a small rock, but I ignored the significance of the rock. Like many people who read the Bible, I focused on the act. I missed the principle the writer was trying to convey in the story: God uses small things to create big change. Saul and the Children of Israel obviously did not know this principle.

King Saul and Israel saw Goliath as a huge problem. They saw themselves as insignificant compared to the giant. As a result, they felt they did not have what it took to defeat such a huge enemy. Like many people who face big problems, they were looking for big solutions. Little did they know the big God they served required proper use of the little things. So, when David came marching on the scene, he did not look like the solution to

Israel's problem. He did not meet the description of an expected hero. David did not look like a warrior, but he was responsible when it came to tasks he was given. He was simply the keeper of the sheep, which some would have considered an insignificant job. However, David risked his life to protect those sheep. He cared for them and loved them with all his heart. What others saw as a minimal task he saw as honorable and important.

When David stepped onto the scene and agreed to fight Goliath, everyone laughed and scorned him. They saw David as a small shepherd boy, not as a strong warrior. Goliath took one look at him and felt insulted. Little did they know David had something they all lacked: a huge heart. The people of Israel and the Philistines failed to realize God doesn't want man's physical strength. However, God does require the use of a big heart. Saul and his men were all great warriors. Saul even looked like a champion, but he had a coward's heart. Anytime he faced a huge problem, he did what most people with small hearts do: he ran away and hid. The story of David and Goliath is more than an epic battle between two nations; it's about how God accomplishes His purpose on Earth. God uses what man considers insignificant to make a big impact. If you read the story carefully, you will notice the attention to detail the writer gives to the characters. The writer goes to great length to describe Goliath's physical size and his advanced weaponry. We are told Goliath's armor weighed five thousand shekels of bronze and the head of his spear alone weighed six hundred shekels of iron. I don't know what any of that really means, but it sure sounds heavy. The writer also tells us that David was small and ruddy. The Israelites were afraid, shaking in their boots. The Bible tells us, *"When Saul and all of Israel heard these words of the Philistine, they were dismayed and greatly afraid."* (1 Samuel 17:11 NIV) King Saul even offered to compensate whomever would go up against the giant. The men still refused to fight. Yet, David came forward and accepted the challenge to fight the giant. They failed to learn an important lesson about their big God: God uses trivial things to solve big problems. In fact, this is a constant theme in the Bible. If you are going to be successful you must find value in what you already possess. You have something of value to offer the world. However, you will never discover it if you too busy complaining about your life.

.

# Stop Complaining and Contribute

*"Be the change you want to see in the world."*
*Mahatma Gandhi*

We read the story of David but never really consider what it meant to be a shepherd. There was often little hope for a shepherd. They were considered low-class people. A shepherd was a dirty job and often reserved for a non-family member. It often entailed shoveling manure and getting dirty. David seized upon an opportunity that no one else wanted. David would have to stay in the heat or the cold protecting the sheep. It was his responsibility to find food for them. This often meant putting himself last. David could have easily complained, and maybe he did. If David complained, it was to God (Psalms). However, he didn't let situations determine his worship and kept his faith in God. He turned an unwanted job into an opportunity. If you are going to be successful at anything, you must learn to create opportunities where there appear to be none. Creators don't complain; they create.

Are you complaining about your job? What if you stopped complaining and looked for the opportunities that exist? If you work in a fast food restaurant, think about the opportunity you have every day to meet new and interesting people. Being a cashier is a wonderful opportunity to develop your people skills. If you are a police officer, you could develop great conflict resolution skills. If you are a nurse, you could practice helping people feel better when they are in pain. Your job may just be the training ground God is using to prepare you for the next level. I didn't know then that all of my years as a detective would make me a great researcher and teacher. Instead of seeing your job as a burden, look at it as a springboard into your purpose. Imagine if David was too busy complaining about being a shepherd when Samuel showed up to anoint him king? He would have complained that he was not fit to be a king. He would have told Samuel he didn't have the experience, or he was too small. Sound familiar? What are you so busy complaining about that is keeping you from hearing God? One way to hear your complaints is to listen to your prayers. Some of our prayers are even complaints to God. We tell God that we need certain things to feel blessed while ignoring the things we already possess. One way to avoid complaining is find to a way to contribute what you have right now. When you stop complaining, a path to your purpose will reveal itself to you, just like it did David.

David did not know that fighting Goliath would be his path to becoming king. He was not promised the throne if he fought Goliath. He just saw an opportunity to glorify God's name. God provides opportunities to those who are willing to bring glory to Him, not those seeking glory for themselves. People who want praise avoid problems and wait until everything seems perfect before they will act. They don't look for these small opportunities, but instead the right opportunity. You want to know what to call a perfect opportunity? A PROBLEM! A problem to you is a PERFECT OPPORTUNITY to God.

Many opportunities will appear in the form of a problem. Problems are opportunities in disguise. Problems draw out the best in us. We are all born as a solution to a problem. God will provide opportunities for us to discover our purpose by allowing us to confront problems. Moses had to confront Pharaoh, David had to fight Goliath, and Jesus had to confront the Pharisees. David became king because he took advantage of the opportunity God provided to him to fight Goliath. David could have tried to plot and to plan his way to the throne. David could have said to himself, "I will wait until Saul is killed in battle and that will be my perfect opportunity to take over as king," but he did not think that way. He saw fighting Goliath as an opportunity to allow God to showcase His power. David was small in stature, but he had something that attracted God: a big heart.

# The Need for a Big Heart

*Do not look at his appearance or the height of his
stature; because I have rejected him, for God sees not as
man sees, for man looks at the outer appearance, but the
Lord looks at the heart. 1 Samuel 16:7*

It was early. My partner and I left the precinct to go get some coffee from Starbucks. The closest one to our office was located in an affluent area. So when we pulled up and saw a homeless guy out front begging for money, we were surprised. I tried to conceal my detective badge behind my suitcoat. I was there to get coffee, not to provide free security. As my partner and I walked past the gentleman, he looked at our badges and began to walk away. The people in the Starbucks looked at us with a sigh of relief as we entered the coffee shop. You could sense the homeless guy made them uneasy. We ordered our coffee and exited. As we were walking back to our vehicle, I heard a voice say, *"Excuse me, Sir?"* I turned around and noticed the homeless guy bowing at the waist, apologizing for interrupting my morning routine. He then proceeded to tell me he was sorry to ask me for money, but he was extremely hungry. He told me he didn't want any trouble. I reached in my pocket to provide him with the change I had left over from my coffee. Before giving him the money, I asked him for his name. Now, this is where things got strange. The guy paused. I assumed he thought I was going to do a background inquiry on his name and check for warrants. But then he started crying. As he wiped his tears, he replied, "Sir, I'm sorry for crying, but no one has ever asked me for my name. I have been homeless for years and people give me money and food, but never has anyone wanted to know my name. My name is Michael." At this point, I had tears in my eyes. I reached into my pocket pulled out my wallet and gave him a five-dollar bill. The man then smiled and said, "You have already made my day by asking my name. Thank you!" I walked away and could not believe such a small gesture could have made such a profound impact. As I drove past the man in my patrol car he yelled across the parking lot, "Sir! You have a big heart." I smiled. Who knew asking someone their name could give them hope?

When I look back at that moment, I still don't know what made me ask the guy his name. I thought it was a small gesture and a decent thing to do. What I considered small was huge to Michael. A man with so little was moved by someone simply wanting to acknowledge him by name. Michael reminded me to be grateful for all things, no matter how small.

Some people despise small gestures, especially when they are in need of something big. In fact, we don't have to be in need to despise trivial things. The only thing we like small is our waistline and our loan balance. Our world is obsessed with finding success and making money. We get excited listening to how celebrities live. We attend seminars and workshops hoping to learn the secrets to success. Our top-rated television shows are about ordinary people competing for stardom. We are so attracted to massive things that we overlook anything small. Although this book is about how to use small things to make big changes, there is one area where you cannot afford to be small. That area is your heart. A big heart is one not full of unresolved pain and unforgiveness.

Unforgiveness and unresolved pain cause our heart to shrink. Life will cause pain, but you must learn to forgive. God can heal a hurt heart but cannot use it. Why? When we have a hurt heart, we protect it, even from God. My point is this: **You must allow God to heal your heart.** God's desire is for us to be healed. It won't be a quick or easy healing like the ones portrayed on television. Although I believe God has the power to heal us instantaneously, I believe His preferred method is to draw us near while we seek healing. God heals us, so we can help others with their own pain. A person with a hurt heart will seek comfort in possessions or titles. They may feel that money or power will make up for their pain. However, they soon learn money and power is no substitute for true healing. We witness this when we see rich and famous people get addicted to drugs, commit crimes, or even take their own lives. The difference between a hurt heart and a healed one is what life means. A hurt heart will view life as unfair and the world as a dangerous place. The healed heart will view life as a gift and recognize the world as a place of possibilities. We do not see with our eyes but with our hearts. If our heart is hurt, it will cause us to hear and see pain. As a result, our eyes become dim to other people's needs. As the Bible warns us, *"Keep your heart with all diligence, for out of it flows the issues of life."* Proverbs 4:23 NIV

You can only use small things to make big change if you have an enormous heart. King David is best known for killing the giant philistine, Goliath. David killed Goliath with a small stone. Why would David choose such an unconventional weapon against such a formidable opponent? The answer is that David had a big heart. While King Saul and others were attempting to get David to use typical weapons like a sword and shield, David didn't see the need for such weapons. When you have a big heart, you don't need big things. Let us consider again the story of David so you can see what I mean.

When God decides to do something on Earth, He always searches for a heart. However, it can't just be any available heart; it must be a courageous one. The story of Israel's most successful king proves this point. The story of King David is a fitting example of how God prefers to use big hearts to accomplish the impossible. In fact, it was the story of David and Goliath that caused me to realize how God can do anything with a big heart. Before reading the story, I was trying to follow God with my mind while still protecting my heart. My heart was broken, and I tried to protect it from everyone, including God.

When our hearts are broken or in pain we go into survival mode. The world is often seen as a dangerous place. Instead of engaging with the world, we retract from it. Life seems difficult with a hurt heart. People often tell you to listen to your heart. But if your heart is hurt, you will not be inclined to listen to it; you will instead protect it.

As a result, we fear the unknown. Like the Children of Israel, we began to depend on external things for safety and comfort.

Israel had gone through a lot. They were in pain and angry. As a result, their hearts had shrunk. Now they wanted a king, not only to have a powerful person to take blame, but also so they could be like other nations. When things went wrong, they could hold the king responsible. A hurt heart is concerned about image.

They were concerned about their image as a nation. They thought a physical king would make them appear safe. However, they chose a king based on his appearance and not heart. The Nation of Israel was about to engage in an epic battle with the Philistines. The Philistines had a giant soldier named Goliath who challenged King Saul to a battle. Instead of fighting Goliath, Saul hid along with his men. Israel's king hid because he wanted to protect his image. He did not want to take a chance when there was a possibility of losing. Israel also hid. It they lost the battle it would be the kings' fault, not theirs.

King Saul was their excuse not to fight. What is your excuse not to fight your giants? Who have you crowned king or queen of your life? Is it your parents? Your troubled childhood? The church? Or do you blame God? We often blame other people or things for our pain to protect our image. Images only matter to people, not to God! God desires our hearts.

Saul looked like a typical king, but did not have the heart of a king. The people of Israel chose Saul to be their king based solely on his image. Saul came from a well-known and wealthy family. They would soon discover, **you can't win spiritual battles with outward beauty.** Often, we look at appearances and make our decisions. The true meaning of blindness is not the inability to see, but the incapability to hear spiritually. You will never win a battle with physical strength or appearance. **ALL BATTLES ARE WON SPIRTUALLY!** Israel had to learn this the hard way.

David knew something that his father and brothers didn't know. He learned early that God desires our heart. God is not interested in our material possessions or abilities. Nor is God interested in your good behavior. Do not equate good behavior with a good heart. ("*And when you pray, do not be like the hypocrites, for they love to pray standing in the synagogues and on the street corners to be seen by others. Truly I tell you, they have received their reward in full.";* Matthew 6:5 NIV.) Sometimes good behavior conceals a broken heart. A good heart is one that is available to God.

God wants a vulnerable heart. David had a malleable heart that God could shape to fit His purposes. The continuous renewal of his heart put David in the right standing with God. God referred to David as a "man after my heart." While he was small in people's eyes, he was big in God's eyes. I don't know about you, but I would rather be big in God's sight than in man's sight. But, I must warn you, a big heart comes with a price.

# A Big Heart Is a Vulnerable One

*My grace is sufficient for you, for my strength is made
perfect in weakness.* 2 Corinthians 12:9

God sent Samuel to anoint David to be
King for one primary reason; David had a big
heart. Although David was a great warrior and
shepherd, it was his heart that attracted God. The
Bible tells us that after *"removing Saul, he made
David their king. God testified concerning him: 'I have
found David, son of Jesse, a man after my own heart; he
will do everything I want him to do"* (Acts 13:22).
God knows that little things become significant
when planted in a big heart. Now, when I say big
heart, I mean one that is malleable. The heart is
like soil. It must be cultivated, maintained, and
softened before it can be used. Pain and fear often
make our hearts hard. When our hearts grow
hard, they shrink. God cannot use this type of
heart. We must allow God to heal our heart, so He
can enlarge it. A healed heart can produce
profound miracles. A small idea can become a life-
changing invention, a dream can turn into a civil
rights movement, and faith as the size of a

mustard seed can move mountains. Notice God said David would do everything He wanted him to do. God often asks us to do what seems humanly impossible. This requires a heart that is willing to face difficulty, uncertainty, and the impossible. It is our hearts that allow God's power to be manifested on the Earth. However, God cannot use a weak heart.

It takes a strong heart to walk with purpose. We often focus on fulfilling our purpose while neglecting to strengthen our hearts. Many of us are not walking in our purpose because we have timid hearts. I have many friends who are depressed because they lack the courage to step out on faith. You too may have people in your life who love their secure, static lifestyles. People often secure fancy degrees and chase after job promotions so they can feel safe. Then, when God asks them to leave everything, their hearts grow faint. Like the rich young ruler in the bible, they turn away from following God and walk away sad. Many of us love to invite God into our lives, but we refuse to be brave. As Hebrews 11:6 teaches us, "Without faith (*brave heart*), it is impossible to please God." What does it mean to be brave? It means giving up your plans and totally trusting God. I admit this can be incredibly frightening. God often takes us through a process in which our faith is tested. We are stripped of our comfort and security. In addition, we are asked to go into areas where we are unfamiliar and have very little control. Success doesn't happen overnight, unless perhaps you win the lottery. However, I don't equate winning the lottery with success. Money doesn't make you successful. Making a positive impact in the world is how you measure success. In order to make any type of positive impact you must go through what David had to endure: a long, arduous process.

## Be Vulnerable

Get rid of your security blanket. It has stopped many people from walking into their purpose. We were taught to crave security and safety from a young age. Vulnerability is seen as weakness in our culture. However, God sees it as strength. It takes a lot of courage to be vulnerable because you must expose your heart. Many of us are afraid of this because we have weak hearts and do not wish to be hurt. This is especially true for men. Most men rely on their physical strength because they want to protect their hearts. Women often fall for these men and then wonder why it is so hard to win their hearts. A man who *always* put on a strong display is just protecting a weak heart.

David was different, and this is what made him special. On the outside he appeared weak, but on the inside David had a vulnerable (strong) heart. The same thing that makes a heart strong is what makes it appear weak: love. Take a look at this familiar scripture again:

*For God so loved the world (His Creation) that he gave his one and only Son (became vulnerable), that whoever believes (becomes vulnerable) in him shall not perish (be weak) but have (strength) eternal life. John 3:16 (emphasis mine)*

Love makes your heart vulnerable. This makes it hard for some people to love. Love puts you at risk of feeling pain. God puts Himself at risk to love the entire world. It sets Him up for unimaginable pain. God understands the power of the heart. Therefore, God only makes Himself vulnerable to those who wish to do the same. When you look at the Ten Commandments, you can see that it looks like God is protecting His heart by setting forth rules that will prevent people from breaking His heart. The first commandment is, *"Thou shall have no other gods before me!"* The second commandment supports the first one, *"You must not make for yourself an idol of any kind or an image of anything in the heavens or on the earth or in the sea."* God knows that love comes with a great risk, but the benefits are worth it.

When Israel wanted a king, it broke God's heart. But God forgave them for their choice. Being vulnerable means even after you have been hurt, you must be able to make your heart available to love once again. Therefore, forgiveness is a must if you are going to be healthy. This will require you to be willing to die. I know health and death shouldn't be mentioned together in the same paragraph. However, this is really what God is asking you to do. Dying to our will awakens us to God's will.

## Focus on Healing; Not Success

Most of us will never fully heal from all the deep wounds that have been inflicted upon us during our lifetime. We have heard that, "Time heals all wounds," but in reality time alone will not heal any wound. Healing is hard work and must be intentional. Healing hurts in the beginning, which is why many people would rather try to just cope with their pain. Healing forces us to stop running and confront our pain. Could it be that your desire for success is really your attempt to escape pain? If so, God wants to begin the healing process in your life. Yes, before you pray for that new car or big house, God wants to heal you. Healing allows God to use your heart to heal others who are hurting. Generally when we are in pain, we want it to go away. God's goal is to heal your pain, not just relieve it. However, before the pain can be removed God must eliminate your painkillers: anger and complaining.

Negative energy, such as complaining, unforgiveness, and bitterness actually prevents healing. When you are angry, you become defensive and can no longer operate in your full capacity. Your spirit becomes blocked and your creativity is stifled. Let me stop and give you a wisdom nugget: You have a social brain. It will operate at its best when involved in social activities. Hence, you must let people into your life if God is going to work through you. The enemy's greatest tactic is to get you angry, isolated, and separated. LISTEN TO ME: If the enemy can separate you from people; God's power is thwarted. God blesses us so we can bless others. Your gifts are meant for other people. The enemy wants you to hate yourself so you can despise others. But remember, we were never meant to be alone.

"The LORD God said, "It is not good for the

man to be alone. I will make a helper suitable (*one whom he can share My Love with*) for him." Genesis 2:18 (emphasis mine)

## Don't Defend your Anger; Listen to it!

*Then the LORD said to Cain, "Why are you angry? Why is your face downcast? ⁷ If you do what is right, will you not be accepted? But if you do not do what is right, sin is crouching at your door; it desires to have you (control your thoughts), but you must rule over it."* Genesis 4:6-7 (emphasis mine)

Have you ever noticed that when you are angry it's harder to think? There is a scientific reason for this. Your brain has two hemispheres: left and right. The left hemisphere is more analytic, and the right is more emotional. The right brain is also known as the survival brain. It is responsible for your survival. Once the right brain gets engaged, the left (thinking brain) shuts down. In other words, the more emotional you get, the less you can think clearly. Emotions are not bad. They have a purpose, which is to help you survive. They also signal you to pay attention to what is happening inside of you. Often times the one emotion we are most comfortable with is anger, because it allows us to blame other people for our feelings. However, anger is not meant to be constant, but, like any other emotion, to point us to the pain inside. When you get angry, you should ask the question, "What is inside of me that is being stirred up?" Once you discover the thing that is causing the anger, then you can let it go and allow healing to happen. God provided us with emotions to heal. But if you contain your emotions, they will eventfully come out in harmful ways. Pent up or unresolved emotions are not only harmful to you but also harmful to those around you, especially those closest to you. The Bible demonstrates this when God addresses Cain about his pent-up emotions. Cain was angry but did not want to examine his heart to know why he was angry. This is why God did not accept his sacrifice. God wanted him to express his anger and let it go. Note that God will not accept an offering given with the wrong heart. Anger blocks positive energy from flowing through you. I meet a lot of angry people. They are often angry over things they have no control over. When bad things happen in the world they blame the government, police, other races, or the devil. If anyone had reason to be angry, it was David. David was overlooked and misused, but we never heard him complain, at least not to man. He may have complained to God. David laid his complaints out before God because he knew God was the only one who could address them. God had to allow David to go through the healing process before He gave him access to the throne. Although David was a man after God's own heart, he was not completely healed. God never adds 'ed' to the word, "heal." We will never heal from everything because we will always be in a state of healing. We see this with David and Bathsheba, which shows that he still had some self-esteem issues. I see people go to church and the pastor or minister will declare them totally healed. They never emphasize that the person has been healed from that ailment or that pain. God still wants to get down to the other stuff that is buried inside of us. So, when God allows something in us to come to the surface, He wants us to confront it, not to ignore it.

*"You will be accepted if you do what is right. But if you refuse to do what is right, then watch out! Sin is crouching at the door, eager to control you. But you must subdue it and be its master."* Genesis 4:7

God came to Cain and gave him an opportunity to release his anger, but Cain wanted to hold on to it. As a result, he lashed out and murdered his brother. Did you catch that revelation? Cain's pent-up anger caused him to hurt someone close to him. Is it possible you cannot have a meaningful relationship with anyone because you are holding onto anger? What are you holding on to that God wants you to release? Is it possible that you are blocking your breakthrough because you are holding on to resentment? Are you attracting negative energy, people, and things in your direction?

## You Must Go Through the Process

David is anointed king in public, but he is made king in private. David attended God's prestigious private school: Wilderness University. Have you ever wondered why God uses the wilderness as a training ground? It is a constant theme throughout the Bible. When you see a pattern in the Bible, pay attention, because it always has significance. Everyone from Moses to Jesus had to experience the wilderness. The wilderness is the process before the promise. In the wilderness there is nothing but sun and desert. Your issues are multiplied. There is no way to assuage your problems. You and your heart become intimate. You began to discover what your heart really desires and fears. The wilderness forces you to question your image and discover your identity. False images cannot survive the wilderness. You must bury your old identity (false image) to make it out of the wilderness alive. Like Israel, those who hold onto their old identity eventfully die in the wilderness. Prior to obtaining the promises of God you must endure a wilderness period. It is here you discover your purpose. David had to get rid of the shepherd boy image before God could identify him as king. Jesus had to get rid of the carpenter image before He could fulfill His mission on Earth. However, Jesus allowed His identity to be hidden in God. Only those with God's heart could identify Him. When Jesus was asked about his identity, He always referred to God: *The Father and I are One!* John 10:30

Walking into your purpose does not happen overnight; it is a process. Success is an outcome, not a reward. David wasn't just anointed the king; he worked to become the king. David was king material because he was willing to fight and struggle on behalf of others. Therefore, God referred to David as a man after His own heart. David did not have a perfect heart but an available one. God does not choose perfect people. Moses was a murderer. David murdered a man and got his wife pregnant. Paul started his career as a bounty hunter chasing down Christians. God wants a heart that can love other people. But before this can occur, you must love yourself. One of the greatest obstacles I had to overcome was loving myself in my present state. I was taught that you had to behave a certain way to be lovable, and I was not sure I fit that mold. This attitude caused me to believe that I was never good enough, even for God. Nothing can be as important as the belief you have in yourself. Be honest, how do you feel about yourself? This is not the time to be untruthful. Be honest! Often we ignore our feelings, believing we can cope and make it through life without feeling. God will often lead us to a place where we cannot rely on our strength, so we must rely on God, which means giving up the one thing we cherish most: Control.

## Untie Yourself –You Cannot Control God

It was a sunny day in Atlanta, Georgia. I sat on my back patio awaiting to take my chicken off the grill. I wanted to get inside because the wind was picking up. I did not want the dirt from the ground to blow into the grill and ruin my meal. It was then I asked myself a crazy question: Where did this wind come from? I couldn't see it or stop it, yet it had a force that could destroy anything in its path. I wondered what made the wind so powerful? Then it hit me: the wind is not attached to anything. What gives the wind its power is the fact that it has no boundaries. I wondered, what if I became like the wind? What if I let go of everything I was holding onto; would I, too, be a force? I wanted to discover what it was like being like the wind. I wanted to soar and be able to remove anything in my path. But first I had to let go. However, in order to let go I had to know what was holding me back. It didn't take me long to figure it out: It was my beliefs. I believed I was not enough. I saw myself as inadequate. This belief was stopping me from moving in the direction God was calling me toward. Is it possible your beliefs are also holding you back? More importantly, is it possible your beliefs are holding God back? Are you trying to control God with your beliefs? Our beliefs not only tie us up, they bound God.

*He could not do any miracles there, except lay his hands on a few sick people and heal them. He was amazed at their lack of faith.* Mark 6:5 NIV

I travel a lot. Each time I get on a plane I am amazed how such a huge machine can get off the ground, let alone soar through the air. I am then reminded of the courage of two men that made this possible: the Wright Brothers. In December 1903, when everyone was still fascinated with the automobile, Orville and Wilbur Wright had the audacity to believe humans could fly. What were the Wright Brothers thinking? They weren't; they were believing. In order to even attempt such an incredible feat, they had to believe it was possible. But more importantly they had to let go of what they already believed.

In order to believe humans could fly, the Wright Brothers had to let go of the belief humans could not fly. Now I know that seems obvious, but it is not easy. It would mean they had to deal with people thinking they were crazy. Then they had to get over their fear of failing -in this case their fear of dying! Many had attempted this same feat but failed. In fact, people far more qualified than the Wright Brothers had even tried and failed. The odds were stacked against them. In addition, they did not have the money to fund their dream. That goes to show you that money doesn't make dreams come true, beliefs do. As the Bible reminds us, *nothing is impossible for the one that believes*. Mark 9:23. It was the Wright Brothers' beliefs that gave them the courage to try the impossible. By letting go of what everyone else believed and following their own beliefs, they were able to soar into the history books. The same thing applies to you and me. If we want to have an impact on the world, we must be willing to let go of some things;

primarily, our beliefs.

### Believe it or not?

*He (Jesus) told them this parable: "No one tears a piece out of a new garment to patch an old one. Otherwise, they will have torn the new garment, and the patch from the new will not match the old. And no one pours new wine into old wineskins. Otherwise, the new wine will burst the skins; the wine will run out and the wineskins will be ruined. No, new wine must be poured into new wineskins. And no one after drinking old wine wants the new, for they say, 'The old is better.'"* Luke 5:36-39 NIV

What determines true success is not what you attract, but what you are willing to let go. Are you committed to a situation that you need to let go of? What about your beliefs? Did you know that your beliefs control your faith in yourself and your trust in God? Believe it or not (no pun intended), your current situation is the result of what you believe. You must untie or detach yourself from your current beliefs if your situation is ever going to change. Many people find this difficult to digest. They don't consider beliefs as hindrances to success. They view this step as being too easy. I remind people that changing your belief system is no small task. It will mean letting go of everything you believed in the past. People who hold onto old, negative beliefs have a tough time believing that most anything is possible. It is not because they don't want to believe, it is because they are attached to their current belief system, which they feel may be beneficial in some way. This helps them explain away their inaction. The faulty belief gives them an excuse for why they are not happy or successful. People like this instead find something or someone to blame. They may even attach themselves to a righteous cause in our society. On the surface, it looks as though they are doing an honorable thing with their life. But if you look closely, they are hiding some resentments. They are angry with the state of their lives and believe they will never be happy. So instead they find something to be unhappy about. At least this way they can join the ranks of people who are unhappy. Now they can be happy about being unhappy. David's brothers did not like him because of his beliefs. How could an illegitimate shepherd boy be anointed king? But it didn't matter what they believed; it mattered what David believed. David believed he was more than a shepherd boy. His belief in himself allowed God to move him where only his beliefs could take him. Learn the lesson God teaches us with David's life: *You will never travel beyond your beliefs.* Let go of your old belief system and align your beliefs with God's destiny for your life. Now, I know the next question is, "How do I know what God's plan is for my life?" I would say start by being honest and admit what you believe about yourself. Do you believe you are a failure? Do you believe you are not enough? If so, ask yourself where these beliefs originated. Your beliefs could be blinding you from knowing your destiny. Here is a clue: Your destiny will always involve helping people in some way. You were born to be a vessel for God's blessings. It is difficult to help others when you believe you are not enough. You will think you have nothing to offer to the world. This is what God calls pride. Pride is not thinking you are too much, but thinking you are too little.

Here is another clue: God will always call you to do something that contradicts your current belief. Wait! Did I just contradict myself? No! David and others had to overcome their own negative beliefs. They did not always believe. I'm sure in the beginning David had difficulty believing he would become king. However, he had to let go of his unbelief (doubt). Letting go of what you belief and adopting what God believes about you is what the Bible refers to as faith. God used David and others in the Bible because of their faith. Their faith allowed God to call them into their purpose. Their faith superseded their condition. Moses was called to be a liberator when he was a fugitive; Abraham was called to be a father when he was fatherless; and David was called to be a king while he was a shepherd. Also notice before each one of them could walk in their purpose they had to let go of what they previously believed. You are no different. Your beliefs could be blinding you from your purpose. God called me to speak to crowds while I was still afraid of people. I could not see God's vision because my belief (voice). Remember, your beliefs are your voice. They guide you. Wait just a minute! You mean to tell me I am not led by my desires? No! You are led by your beliefs. Go ahead, name something you have a passion for right now. Now, stop and identify the belief behind the desire. You see I had no passion to speak to crowds because I believed I had nothing of value to say. God never calls you by your passion. If He did, we would all be rich. Before you hear God's call, your beliefs must align with His purpose.

Many people say your purpose will be something you have a passion for doing. You can have a passion for fishing or bowling—but that doesn't mean it is your purpose. Your purpose will often involve how you will help make the world better for other people. So, the question is not what do you love? The question should be, what do you believe? If you want to move toward your dreams you must discover what you believe. Then you must determine if your beliefs are keeping you from being successful. I must warn you, however, that this is no easy task.

Letting go of what we believe is just as important as obtaining a new belief. In fact, all new beliefs must compete with old ones. Our existence is rooted in what we believe. Our actions reflect what we believe. This can be a good thing or a terrible thing. Arguments and wars have been started simply because of belief systems. A person who believes we should eradicate homelessness will commit their existence to changing the world's homeless situation. A person who believes other races do not deserve equal rights will commit their lives to prove themselves right. Religious beliefs govern people's decisions. Our entire lives align with our beliefs. Once we submit to a belief, it is difficult to accept new ones. This embedded belief is often referred to as a "core" belief. A core belief is how you see yourself in the world. If you have accepted the belief you don't deserve a good life, you will not only hold onto the belief, but you will even defend it. Anything or anyone that contradicts the belief will be considered suspicious or untrustworthy. For instance, I grew up with the belief I wasn't good enough. It didn't matter how many good things people said about me. One bad statement would erase every compliment I ever received. Why? Because the bad statement aligned with what I already believed about myself. The good statements contradicted what I believed. I also grew up believing that anything bad that happened to me was God punishing me. The belief made me afraid of God. I believed I could never be good enough to deserve God's love. As a result, I was in constant search of proof of my worth. It is important that you be honest about your beliefs. If you are not sure what you believe, take a look at your life. How did you end up where you are today? If you are honest, your core belief will reveal itself. But why are core beliefs so powerful?

Your old belief or core belief holds more power, because it has already occurred. The new belief has yet to be proven and often has no support. I have found the best way to understand your belief is to observe how you respond to life's challenges. When we face challenges, we are forced to look inside and rely on what we believe. Challenges show us what we already believe.

Many of us run from challenges because they confront our core beliefs. For instance, I worked in the police department for twenty years and never sought a promotion. Even when I did take the test for promotion, I never studied or put forth much effort. People would always encourage me to take the test. They said I would make a great leader. However, this contradicted what I believed about myself. As a result, I spent twenty years never pursuing a promotion because I believed I was not good enough. I had to let go of this belief if I was ever going to find further success. Notice I didn't say, "I had to change this belief." Beliefs cannot be changed; they can only be replaced. Changing beliefs is like putting on a clean shirt over a dirty one; the dirty one will always be closer to your heart.

God does not want to compete with anything in your life. He wants to rule. Anything you do in life will either align or compete with your beliefs. God will wait until your old beliefs depart before speaking to you. It is difficult for God to hear an unbelievers prayer; *"**And without faith it is impossible to please God**, because anyone who comes to him must believe that he exists and that he rewards those who earnestly seek him."* Hebrews 11:6 NIV. It is not because God does not want to hear your prayers. He just doesn't want to pour new wine into old wineskins. Do me a favor: Write down your current beliefs and write down what you want to accomplish throughout your life. Then be honest with yourself. Do you think your accomplishments will change your beliefs about yourself? If so, chances are, you have a faulty belief system. Situations don't change beliefs; beliefs change situations. Changing beliefs will often involve you being uprooted and moved to unfamiliar territory.

Stop and listen. What are you saying with your life? Is your life boring? Do you dread getting up each morning? What do you believe about your life? The answer to these questions can give you a clear picture of your future. Beliefs determine the course of our lives. Our beliefs are unspoken declarations. We communicate these declarations subconsciously through our daily choices. As a result, our life mirrors our beliefs. The universe is like a sounding board. It will bring you what you communicate. If you believe you are inadequate, you will settle for anything life brings your way. You will see challenges as obstacles, failure as a death sentence, and the accumulation of material things as success. The things that matter most, like family, friends and relationships, will have little value. So, before we continue, let me ask you another question.

Are you willing to leave where you are and go where you have never been? Are you willing to be comfortable being uncomfortable? Well, this is what it takes to be successful in your purpose. You must be willing to depart from your current life to journey where God wants to take you. You see this throughout the Bible. Abraham, Moses, and David all had to leave their former lifestyles to fulfill their purpose. You will have to do the same. In fact, it is one of the first things God will ask you to do. If you cannot detach yourself, God cannot use you. Remember the rich young ruler in the Bible?

*Just then a man came up to Jesus and asked, "Teacher, what good thing must I do to get eternal life?"*

*"Why do you ask me about what is good?" Jesus replied. "There is only One who is good. If you want to enter life, keep the commandments."*

*"Which ones?" he inquired.*

*Jesus replied, "'You shall not murder, you shall not commit adultery, you shall not steal, you shall not give false testimony, honor your father and mother,'[a] and 'love your neighbor as yourself.'[b]"*

*"All these I have kept," the young man said. "What do I still lack?"*

*Jesus answered, "If you want to be perfect, go, sell your possessions and give to the poor, and you will have treasure in heaven. Then come, follow me."*

*When the young man heard this, he went away sad, because he had great wealth.*

Matthew 19:16-22 NIV

The young man had everything. But his beliefs stopped him from making a decision to follow Jesus. He did not think he was not good enough without his material possessions. He wanted to follow Jesus because he believed Jesus would add even more value to him. Jesus told the rich young ruler to go sell all his belongings. I'm sure if Jesus would have stopped there, the young ruler would have been okay with the proposition. But Jesus went further and told the ruler to give the proceeds from his estate sale to the poor. Then Jesus gave him the final part of the deal: follow him (leave what you are familiar with). The Bible says the rich young ruler went away sad. I want you to pay attention to how the Bible describes this man. He seemed to have everything life could offer him. He was rich, young, and a ruler. He was also attached to these titles. His belief was that his value was attached to the things he owned. It wasn't the things he was not able to leave behind - it was his belief, a belief that would not allow him to follow Jesus. What belief are you holding onto that has you stuck in your current situation? Are you too attached to your current beliefs? You must discover your core belief because it will determine how you see yourself and the world. Your core belief determines your vision. And it is your vision that will ultimately lead you to your purpose.

# Get Your Vision Checked

*Whenever the Israelites saw the man, they all fled from him in great fear. Now the Israelites had been saying, "Do you see how this man keeps coming out? He comes out to defy Israel. The king will give great wealth to the man who kills him. He will also give him his daughter in marriage and will exempt his family from taxes in Israel."*1 Samuel 17:24-25

Saul and the Israelites ran and hid from Goliath. It wasn't that Goliath was a big giant; it was more how small they saw themselves in comparison. God could not use them because they saw themselves as inadequate. This was not the first time the power of God was crippled by blurred vision. In Numbers 13 we read, "We saw the Nephilim there (the descendants of Anak come from the Nephilim). We seemed like grasshoppers in our own eyes, and we looked the same to them." Their vision was obstructed by negative beliefs. Notice, I did not say doubt. There is no such thing as doubt; you belief something. What we call doubt is really faulty beliefs. The next time you doubt something, ask yourself, "What faulty belief am I entertaining." Don't just ask the question. Listen to your answer.

Remember: Vision is determined by how we hear ourselves. If you are going to be successful in anything, you will need proper vision. Many people wake up every morning and just wander aimlessly. They have no clue what they want to do with their lives or why. A vision is a picture of how you want to use your time here on Earth. Your vision guides your decisions and choices. Some people refer to it as your dream, but I prefer the term "vision." Vision points to a direction. It is your vision that determines your direction and how you want to use your life. For instance, my vision is to educate the world on the effects of abuse. I want to use my life to make the world better and free from abuse. My vision guides all my decisions. It determines how I spend my time, what I read, my financial decisions, and who I allow to come into my life. In order for me to see this vision, I have to hear God's voice directing me. God's voice will not compete with mine. My voice or what I say about myself must align with what God says about me; this is what I mean by vision. Supporting God's vision is what we call PROVISION.

Without a vision, you will wander aimlessly

through life. You will waste your time on social media, hanging out, watching television, or just lounging around the house. Now don't get me wrong, nothing is wrong with any of these things in moderation. But if that is all your life consists of, then you will accomplish very little with your life. You were born to make a difference in the world. You are not here just to live and eventually die. You were sent to Earth with a purpose. You must find a way to use that purpose to make the world a better place.

Now I know someone will say, "But Kevin, I work at McDonald's as a cashier, how can I make the world better?" I would say, find a problem in the world where you believe you can reasonably make a difference. Then ask yourself what is unique about your life that enables you to bring change to this problem. Next, find a way to get involved. Notice I never mentioned how much money you can make from doing so. In fact, I would say find a way to give, without considering the gains.. Do not consider any gains. What you are looking for here is meaning, not money. You may volunteer your time or set aside a couple of dollars a month to donate. By doing this you have automatically added meaning to your job. You no longer work to get paid, but you work so you can contribute to help solve a problem. You have become a change maker by taking what you have in your hand and using it for good. You are no longer someone who complains about the world's problems, instead you have now become a solution to the world's problems. Although this will seem small to you, it is big in God's sight. Once God see you are a leader of little things, God can then trust you with even bigger things.

Another thing will happen once you get a sharp vision. You will no longer be distracted by things that have nothing to do with your vision. Your life will become clearer. It will be easier to make decisions regarding your time, finances, and relationships. Prior to having a vision, I joined every get-rich-quick scheme you could imagine. I listened to every person who made a promise to make me successful. I read self-help books. I played the lottery hoping to get rich. I was all over the place. My email was filled with people promising to help me be happy and have a better life. Once I was clear on how I wanted to impact the world, none of those things mattered. I only read things that helped me with my vision. I became less interested in what was on television or what was happening on social media. I became focused. As a result, a whole new world opened up to me. I no longer waited for change, I created it. I was on my way to helping the world get better.

Your vision should involve two things. It should be something that makes the world better, and it should be something you cannot accomplish alone. Yes, David singlehandedly defeated Goliath, but it took the rest of Israel to defeat the Philistine Army. You can lead the charge, but you will need others to complete the mission. In short, your vision should be bigger than yourself. Your vision can be anything, but I have discovered it is normally something you care about or have been personally affected by. For example, my desire to eradicate the world of abuse came from me being a victim myself. When I was twelve years old, I was kidnapped and sexually assaulted by a strange man. Once the man was done assaulting me, he attempted to kill me. I fought him off and ran all the way home. I lied to my mom and told her I was robbed. I was too embarrassed to admit my first time having sex was with a man I never knew. Growing up I never told anyone. I kept it a secret until I was in my forties – just a few years ago. It took me a long time to realize my vision. Why? I was too busy complaining about my life. I didn't see my life as an opportunity to help other victims. Once my perspective changed, so did my life. My vision became clear and I could see my path to my purpose.

Your vision should always include a plan on how to make the world better. It shouldn't be just for personal gain. I have discovered people who have a vision want to contribute something to the world. People confuse vision with desire. We desire goods and people to make us happy. Looking for happiness will cause you to navigate life with your physical eyes. People who want to be happy are led by images not vision.

## Stop Searching for Happiness

"The key to realizing a dream is to focus not on success but on significance—and then even the small steps and little victories along your path will take on greater meaning." Oprah Winfrey

I was excited. Oprah Winfrey was coming to Atlanta with her "The Life You Want Weekend Tour". I made sure I got my tickets early. As soon as my check hit the bank, I took my 200 dollars and purchased tickets. I could only afford the cheap seats, but nothing associated with Oprah is actually cheap. I would need a magnifying glass to see, but at least I would be in the building. I felt it was a couple of hundred dollars well spent. Who would not want to see Oprah in person? Plus, she was traveling with some of the most influential people on the planet. People I admired. I would get to listen to Deepak Chopra, Iyanla Vanzant, Elizabeth Gilbert, Rob Bell, and Mark Nepo. I had read all their books and followed their work. Now I would be able to see and hear them live. I was excited. I was riding on cloud nine! Well, that is, until my phone rang. I answered it and before I could share my excitement I heard a female voice on the other end saying, "Kevin, what are you getting in to?"

It was Wendy, a friend of mine. She called to ask what I was doing for the weekend. I told her I was going to see Oprah and suggested she come with me. She declined. Wendy told me it was a waste of money. We both joked how I would be the only male at the event. I told her I never even considered that. I thanked her for reminding me of my great decision to surround myself with beautiful and ambitious women. I inquired about her plans. Wendy let out a big shout, "Party!" She told me she and some friends were flying to Las Vegas to attend a singles event. Wendy went on to talk about the opportunity she would have meeting successful single men. She said it would be a weekend to remember. She boasted about their delightful hotel room. I asked her how much all this cost. She replied, "Oh we got a deal. It only cost me nine-hundred dollars." I chuckled. She asked why I was laughing. "Just a minute ago you berated me and told me I was wasting two-hundred dollars to go see Oprah and her millionaire friends. Now you tell me that you are spending nine hundred dollars on a weekend of fun." She replied, "But, yeah, at least I will be happy and having fun." I responded, "Yes, but I will have invested in me while you spent nine hundred dollars to be happy. I didn't know happiness was so expensive." And with that, we said our goodbyes. Our friendship eventually ended because we were simply on different paths. She was searching for happiness; I was looking to make an impact in the world. Years later, I bumped into her and she told me she was not happy. She asked if I could give her some advice on happiness. I said, "Yes, stop looking for it, create it."

Happiness is an illusion. It is not an object . You get to decide what happiness looks like for you. A day on the beach is happiness for some people, while others need money and fame. A nice book, a cup of coffee, and a quiet evening is happiness for me. You create your own happiness. You don't have to look for it. When we chase happiness, we lose sight of what's important. Searching for happiness can prevent us from seeing beyond our current condition. It can make us judgmental of ourselves and of others. We can see ourselves as inadequate. It is measuring ourselves that leads to unhappiness. When this happens, nothing will ever be enough; not even paradise.

*"When the woman saw that the fruit of the tree was good for food and pleasing to the eye, and also desirable for gaining wisdom, she took some and ate it. She also gave some to her husband, who was with her, and he ate it. 7 Then the eyes of both of them were opened, and they realized they were naked; so they sewed fig leaves together and made coverings for themselves."* Genesis 3:6-7

Did you notice what happened? Adam and Eve were living in paradise and still were unhappy. They had an unlimited supply of food, no sickness, no crime, and no worries. However, because they believed they were not enough, nothing was sufficient for them. When we think we are not enough, nothing will ever be enough for us. They thought having more would bring happiness, but it only brought more unhappiness. This is what the story of Adam and Eve teaches us—happiness is not something we obtain but something we create. However, we miss this message because when we think of the Garden of Eden; we usually reference sin. The sin was not in taking the fruit; the sin was them not recognizing their worth. They thought they were forbidden so they partook in what did not belong to them. It was their eyes looking for something they already had the power to create. When we use our eyes, we begin to measure ourselves. We look at what others have, and what we do not. This leads to depression. We then began to complain about our lives, which ultimately leads to feelings of unhappiness. The unhappiness stems from your spirit knowing you are not living an authentic existence. Are you living a life that doesn't belong to you? Are you a king or queen living a shepherd's life?

Can you imagine how David would have felt if he were comparing his life to his brothers? He would have been too busy feeling sorry for himself when Samuel came to anoint him king. David allowed himself to be anointed in the presence of his enemies. As someone who was rejected all his life, he could have used it to boast. Yet we do not hear one word of boasting. And to make matters worse, David had to wait years to take the throne. You see, David wasn't searching for happiness, he was searching for significance. If happiness was his goal he would not have wanted to wait on God's timing. When things did not go his way, he would have simply given up. Fighting

Goliath would have been more about him proving himself than about glorifying God. When your goal is to have an impact, you realize that success is not a destination but a journey.

## Don't Leap; Climb

In 2016 comedian, businessman, and television host Steve Harvey spoke to his Family Feud audience about success. He stipulated that success required being willing to take a risk. Steve told his audience that success requires you to jump. He stated you must be willing to take a jump of faith into the unknown. He stated when you do so, your God-given gift will open like a parachute. Steve warned, though, that the parachute might not open immediately. The audience was then told the parachute must open at some point and when it does, you will soar into the life you always wanted. The message was taped and uploaded to YouTube. It didn't take long before it went viral. It inspired millions. People all over the world were talking about the video. In fact, the video became so popular that Steve decided to publish a book expounding on the concept. The book, *Jump: Take the Leap of Faith to Achieve Your Life Abundance*, became a best seller. The book even inspired me to take the leap. However, I discovered the concept of leaping can be a bit misleading.

## The God of the Mountain

In high school, geography was one of my least favorite subjects. Outside my hometown of Memphis and other places like Texas, California, and Hawaii, I could not tell you where anything was located on a map. So, when I was told I would be traveling to Salt Lake City, Utah, I had to Google its location. Besides giving me information, Google gave me a snapshot of what Salt Lake City would look like. The pictures on the Internet did it no justice. I understood why some people referred to Salt Lake City as one of America's most beautiful cities. The views are breathtaking. The city is filled with beautiful, snowcapped mountains. People from all over travel there to hike and ski. Driving up the mountains to one of the many ski resorts can be intimidating and exciting at the same time. One morning, while eating breakfast at the Snowbird Ski Resort restaurant, I noticed a couple of hikers. As I looked out the huge windows, I thought to myself, "Who would risk their life climbing a mountain?" I couldn't think what attracted people to mountain climbing. Maybe it's the thrill of conquering such a huge feat or maybe the spectacular views you get once you get to the top.

I never saw mountain climbing as a fun thing. However, I discovered that climbing mountains takes a lot of courage.

Mountain climbing is a lot like success. In fact, climbing a mountain is more of an accurate metaphor for success than leaping from one. When you climb a mountain, you have no idea what obstacles or challenges await you. If you leap, you just go with the flow; there is very little decision making. Mountain climbing is also different from leaping in that you have to ponder certain questions. What if you got to the other side and were disappointed? I asked a similar question before resigning from my job. Leaving the unfamiliar isn't a leap; it is an uphill battle. I realized I wasn't taking a leap. I was about to go for a climb.

The leap metaphor denotes that all you must do is jump and allow the wind to catch you. In the mountain metaphor, you must look at the obstacle in front of you. Then you must ask yourself, "Am I prepared to take such a risk?" With the leap metaphor, you just jump and pray like hell that your gifts and talents rescue you from a deadly fall. The mountain metaphor allows you to imagine the obstacles. You get to decide if you are willing to take the necessary risks to improve the view of your life. You also get to decide what equipment you will need to make your climb. As you climb, you learn how badly you want what you are chasing. Nothing teaches you more about inner strength and determination than a climb up a mountain. Everything changes when you ascend the slippery slopes. There are falling rocks (setbacks) that can knock you down, forcing you to start over. Once you get past the rocks, you must deal with the dangerous creatures (competition) who call the mountain home. The mountain provides very little shelter (security) from the elements. The air (evidence) up there is also hard to breathe (relax). You must endure the climb (loneliness) all the way to the top. It doesn't get easier. Even if you start off with people, there is no guarantee that they will make it to the top with you. Some people will lose hope and quit, while others will try to talk you out of your mission. Moses, Abraham, Jesus, and even David had to endure the mountains:

*The LORD descended to the top of Mount Sinai and called Moses to the top of the mountain.*
Exodus 19:20 NIV

*Then God said, "Take your son, your only son,*

*whom you love—Isaac—and go to the region of Moriah. Sacrifice him there as a burnt offering on a mountain I will show you."* Genesis 22:1-2 NIV

*After he(Jesus) had dismissed them, he went up on a mountainside by himself to pray. Later that night, he was there alone* Matthew 14:23 NIV

*Saul was going along one side of the mountain, and David and his men were on the other side, hurrying to get away from Saul. As Saul and his forces were closing in on David and his men to capture them.* I Samuel 23:26 NIV

As you can see, the mountain is a tool God uses to train those who wish to obtain an elevated level of success. If you still feel like you want to jump, go ahead, but make sure you pack a pair of hiking boots.

## Be Curious, Ask Questions, and Listen

*"Now Moses was tending the flock of Jethro, his father-in-law, the priest of Midian, and he led the flock to the far side of the wilderness and came to Horeb, the mountain of God. There the angel of the LORD appeared to him in flames of fire from within a bush. Moses saw that though the bush was on fire it did not burn up. So Moses thought, "I will go over and see this*

*strange sight—why the bush does not burn up."*

*When the LORD saw that he had gone over to look, God called to him from within the bush, "Moses! Moses!"*

*And Moses said, "Here I am."*
Exodus 3:1-4

As we drove down the long boring highway, the car grew quiet. I was driving from Memphis back to Atlanta. I had my mom, aunt, and fiancé with me. I assumed everyone in the car was asleep when I heard my mom ask, "Who planted all those trees?" I looked out the window and saw all the trees she was referring to lining the road. It was a forest. I chuckled. I told my mom, "Mom, no one planted those trees, they were there when God created the Earth." She laughed and said, "Well, God planted the trees. You can't consider God a no one." I didn't know how to respond. I was focused on getting home, while my mom was curious about the journey. I was looking with my eyes; she was looking with her heart. My mom was amazed at all the beautiful trees aligned along the road. Her curiosity took her beyond the car. My mom made me pay attention to something I had always ignored. I had driven that route many times and not once did I pay attention to the trees.

I was so focused on my destination, I ignored the beauty of the journey. My mom reminded me of one of life's most important lessons: Learn to listen to the questions in your heart. Life can make us seek answers and miss the beauty right in front of us. Questions are what make life beautiful; not the answers. Questions draw us out and allow us to experience the world. A person who never asks questions will never experience life as the answer. Praying to God should be about questions, not simply seeking answers. God, what do you want me to do with my life? God, who do you want to bless with my gift? God, which mountain shall I climb? Prayer is not seeking answers. It is asking God questions. We often pray with the answer we want in mind. When that answer doesn't manifest, we get disappointed and lose faith. Rarely do we become curious and ask what life is trying to teach us. We engage our hearts when we become curious.

Look at your life right now. If you had to guess, what would you think your life is telling you? When asked this, most people look at their financial status, dating life, employment, or health. Few people look inward. What do I mean by inward? What do you think of yourself? Do you think you are not good enough? Where do these thoughts originate? You must discover this because your life is a direct reflection of your thoughts or the questions you refuse to ask. Let me explain.

# A Thoughtful Life

*Your beauty should not come from outward adornment, such as elaborate hairstyles and the wearing of gold jewelry or fine clothes. Rather, it should be that of your inner self, the unfading beauty of a gentle and quiet spirit, which is of great worth in God's sight.*
1 Peter 3:3-4 NIV

Growing up, my height hindered me from a lot of activities, including making friends. Rarely was I chosen for any competitive sports, like football or basketball. I had few friends throughout elementary school and was often stuck playing imaginary games like "Cops and Robbers." I was always chosen to be the cop. My friends didn't think I made a good criminal because of my size. During our imaginary pursuits, I never apprehended anyone. Maybe that's why I grew up to become a cop in real life. It's ironic how other people's perception of us can determine what we believe about ourselves.

After a while I learned to accept my height. Well, that was until I got beat up by a female twice my size. I felt like I deserved it; she was trying to have a conversation with me and I was being short (pun intended) with her. Afterward, we became best friends. I needed her protection from the bullies. As the years passed, I wished I could say I found something creative to compensate for my size, like sports. I tried playing football, thinking I could use my small size to my advantage. However, I was often left on the sidelines watching others have fun. Again, I came up short. My height wasn't my only problem. I also had to deal with degrading remarks about my appearance. In addition to being small, I had unusually big feet. I would often get teased about the size of my feet. Friends and family members called me Captain Caveman. As a result, I thought very little of myself (there goes that belief again).

As I got older, my height really made me self-conscious, especially around girls. It shaped how I saw myself. I saw my height as a curse. I grew up with the belief that bigger was better and small meant inadequate. As I grew older, this belief guided my life. I subconsciously attempted to compensate for my height by enlarging my image. I paid for expensive clothing, cars, gadgets, and attended get rich quick conferences. I thought that if I made it big, my life would improve. Of course, the only thing that grew bigger was my amount of debt. Do you see what happened? A belief planted in my childhood manifested itself in my adult life. Many times, our bodies grow but our beliefs remain the same. We become adults with childish beliefs. If we do not question our beliefs throughout life, we will become a prisoner to what we believe. I agree with author Alice Miller, who states, *"Our childhood lasts a lifetime."* Meaning, we rarely grow up. Our bodies just get bigger. Honestly, I believe God never meant for us to grow up. I believe God planted all our wisdom in our childlike faith. This why I think it is so important to protect children. They hold the wisdom to our future. By abusing children we destroy our future. *"Truly I tell you, unless you change and become like little children, you will never enter the kingdom of heaven."* Matthew 18:3 NIV Like me, many of us search for meaning in heroic stories.

So, it was no surprise that when I heard the story of David I felt intrigued. I could relate to David. In many ways I wished I had his courage. Despite his physical size, David was not afraid of anything. It was David's bravery that catapulted him to the throne, not his stature. The people saw David's physical size, but God saw David's heart. *"The LORD does not look at the things people look at. People look at the outward appearance, but the LORD looks at the heart."* (NIV I Samuel 16:7) Our heart is where we hide everything, including our pain. Here is where things get tricky. God also hides things in your heart. Have you noticed God often hides the greatest gifts in the smallest places? Diamonds, gold, oil, and pearls are all hidden in difficult-to-reach places. If you desire to get to these valuables, you must be determined and willing to work for them. You must endure the pain and uncertainty of the search. It is the only way you will believe in yourself. God knew this truth. It is why God hid your purpose (treasure) in your heart, right next to your pain. *"For where your treasure is, there your heart will be also."* Matthew 6:21 NIV. Many of us will never discover our purpose (treasure) because we are constantly running from our pain. Then there are those of us who look outside ourselves to find comfort. If you look on the outside, you will never discover the treasure within. You must be willing to confront your pain to get to it. How do you confront your pain? Listen to your thoughts.

Israel had a history of enslavement. As a result, they thought very little of themselves. So, when they faced a big challenge they immediately became afraid. Their thoughts led to fear and it controlled all their decisions; even their decision for a king. The people of Israel would never have chosen David as their king. When the prophet

Samuel was sent to anoint Israel's new king, he never would have chosen David. Samuel was looking to anoint a king based on appearance. However, Samuel had what others did not; a vision. He had the ability to hear God's voice direct him. David would not have been Samuels choice for king. He was small, and didn't look like a king. If fact, he probably didn't come across even as a good shepherd. And most importantly, he was the eighth son of a man who did not even acknowledge him as a son. But, it wasn't up to Samuel or the people. It was up to God. Your life's purpose is between you and God. The story of David gives us a glimpse of how God operates. Why would God choose the least likely of all the people in Israel to become king? The same reason He chose you for your purpose; to change the world. Israel wanted a big king but had to learn; God uses small things to test our faith.

How about you? Do you ever see yourself as being inadequate? If so, you must change how you see yourself. Physical size does not matter to God. It is the size of your faith that pleases God.

*If you had faith; even if it were as small as a mustard seed, you would say to this mountain, move from here to there, and it will move, and nothing will be impossible for you.* Matthew 17:20 ESV

Faith is big in God's eyes, even if it comes in a small quantity. You may be wondering how you know if you have faith. The answer is simple. It is how you treat the little things. God honors those who are faithful with the little things entrusted in their hands. People with no faith need proof of God's existence in their lives. A person of faith will see whatever God gives them as sufficient to accomplish the tasks at hand. God often tests our faith by seeing how responsible we are with small things, before entrusting us with more.

David's life reflects this truth. Although others saw David as being small in every way, he did not see himself as being small; nevertheless, he understood his mindset was no small deal. It was one of the few things David kept big. Therefore, God chose him to be king of Israel. He was a guy with a big heart. Big-hearted people cherish things that may, on the surface, appear little, while people with small hearts cherish grandiose things. David believed he was "king material" even when others saw him just as a simple shepherd boy. God would not have anointed David as king had David not seen himself as a king material. David had to learn that Samuel anointed him, but God had to make him king. When Samuel anointed David king, it was one small step, but he had a lot to learn before taking the throne.

God does not see as man sees, because His ways are not our ways, even though He created us in His image. It is the little things that matter to God. How we respond to the little things will determine how far we get in life. Everything from a child to a plant starts with a small seed. The person who does not see the importance of the little things will never see big changes in his or her life. They will complain about the big things not coming in their direction because they ignored the small ones. Big things get our attention but small things change our lives. However, when God wants our attention He interrupts us in our path.

## Pay Attention to Life's Interruptions

*Now Moses was tending the flock of Jethro his father-in-law, the priest of Midian, and he led the flock to the far side of the wilderness and came to Horeb, the **mountain of God**. There an angel appeared to him in flames of fire from within a bush. Moses saw that the bush was on fire and did not burn up. So Moses thought, "I will go over and see this strange sight— why the bush does not burn up. "*

*When the Lord saw that he had **gone over to look**, God called him from within the bush, "Moses, Moses!"*

*And Moses said, **"Here I Am!"***

Exodus 3:1-4 NIV

I was fatigued. I was at the airport to catch a five-hour flight to a speaking engagement in Portland, Oregon. As I got comfortable waiting at the gate I closed my eyes, hoping to catch a quick nap before my flight. I stared up at the board and noticed that my flight had been delayed. I sighed. I was tired and wanted to get to my destination, check into my hotel, and get some sleep. However, it appeared I would have to wait. I calmed down and began reading. That is when I heard, "Will the following passenger please report to the customer service desk: Kevin McNeil." I looked up to make sure I wasn't hearing things, and then my name was called again. I cautiously approached the customer service desk and identified myself as Kevin McNeil. The attendant informed me he had to put me on another plane because I was not going to be able to make my connecting flight due to the delayed departure time. He told me I would have to catch a flight to St. Louis, then continue on to Las Vegas, before making it to my final destination. I was not happy, but I had no choice. As he printed off my new boarding pass, I could feel my anger building. I was about to learn another important lesson from God: When life interrupts your plans, don't get mad, get focused.

When things don't go your way, don't just get angry; pay attention. The interruption could be God trying to get you to see what is happening around you. For instance, my delayed flight had a purpose. God had a message to deliver to me. When I finally arrived at my destination, I was looking for a sign and was ready to listen. That is when my Uber driver showed up. He was a weird looking white guy with his fingernails painted black. He took my bags and told me to sit up front. Though typically I don't sit up front in an Uber, at this point, I was too tired to make a decision. I just wanted to get to the hotel and get some rest. I had to speak in a couple of hours. As we drove off, he told me he was glad to have me as a passenger and introduced himself as Matthew. He asked me why I was visiting Portland. I told him I was the keynote speaker at a child abuse conference. Matthew then began to tell me he was a marketing expert and real estate agent. He began to share with me some great marketing strategies for my business. Matthew was just the person I had been looking for to improve my reach and spread my message. Now, imagine if I was still upset about my flight being delayed. I would have had an attitude. I would have declined to sit in the front seat, and Matthew would have sensed my animosity. He probably would have thought I was a butthole, and he would have never spoken to me and revealed these marketing secrets.

God may interrupt our daily routines to deliver us a message. Often, we do not recognize these interruptions, because they can be annoying or unexpected.

Interruptions are God's way of getting our attention. What is happening in your life right now that seems like a problem or interruption? What lesson can be learned from it instead?

Are you thinking too small? The problem or interruption you are complaining about may just be an opportunity in disguise. It seems impossible that David ever thought he was going to be king. David's own father didn't even recognize him as a son. He was in a horrible situation. His future was looking hopeless. David was doomed and a failure in everyone's eyes. Well, everyone except God. I also want you to notice God interrupts people who are willing to work.

Noah was interrupted and told to build an ark. Abraham was interrupted and told he would be the father of nations. Moses was on the back side of the desert when God interrupted him and spoke through a burning bush. David was tending sheep when he was interrupted and told to get prepared, so the prophet Samuel could anoint him to be king. If these men had seen interruptions as problems, they would have missed the great opportunity to be used by God. They would have also missed another lesson: God will use past failure to lead you to a future success.

## See Failure as Opportunity

Often when things get interrupted and don't go our way, we think dreadful thoughts. We use our past experiences to assume we will fail in the moment. We forget to bless God for the things we already possess. If we don't appreciate God for the little things, we will definitely not show our appreciation for the big ones. We see ourselves as failures when we don't have what we think we need to make us successful. As a result, we condemn ourselves and stop trying, instead of seeing failure as a second chance to start over. God will allow you to fail. Yes, I know you do not want to hear that statement, but it is true. God will sometimes test you with failure before He allows you to experience success. God wants to see how you handle failure. How you handle failure is a big deal in God's mind. Moses' first attempt to free the Israelites was a failure. Pharaoh rejected his first request to let the people go. This was even after God sent him! Abraham tried repeatedly to have a child after God told him he would be the father of many nations, but again he failed.

Even David failed before taking the throne of Israel when he and his men lost everything, and their wives were taken captive. If you notice, most successful people understand that failure is part of the process. Oprah Winfrey was fired from a news network; author J.K. Rowling of Harry Potter fame was a broke single parent on welfare; Motivational speaker and life coach, Lisa Nichols, was a single parent struggling to take care of her son. These people had to experience failure and handle it properly before they were truly prepared to handle any level of success.

Your journey to success will be no different. Let me say this more plainly: you will fail! However, failures do not come to discourage you. They come to increase your faith. *"These have come so that the proven genuineness of your faith, of greater worth than gold, which perishes even though refined by fire, may result in praise, glory, and honor when Jesus Christ is revealed."* 1 Peter: 7-9 NIV. Failure often exposes what we believe. When you fail you will either give up or find another way to accomplish your goals. Failure increases your willingness to fight for what you believe. Yes, like David you must be willing to face insurmountable odds to be the king or queen of your life. Wait! Did I just call you royalty? Yes, I did! It means you are subject to a sovereign being. David understood this principle. It did not matter what man thought of him. David knew his identity. Failure is another way God draws out our identity. Prior to fighting Goliath, David was provided with many opportunities to fail. Listen to what David tells Saul before fighting Goliath:

*But David said to Saul, "Your servant has been keeping his father's sheep. When a lion or a bear came and carried off a sheep from the flock, [1] went after it, struck it and rescued the sheep from its mouth. When it turned on me, I seized it by its hair, struck it and killed it. Your servant has killed both the lion and the bear; this uncircumcised Philistine will be like one of them, because he has defied the armies of the living God.*
1 Samuel 16:34-36 (NIV)

Notice how confident David is when facing a challenge. This was a result of him overcoming failure and learning to trust in God and his ability. Now, I know what you're saying, that David never mentioned he failed. Of course, he didn't, because successful people rarely do. Once asked, however, they will tell you they had to learn to face failure. It is how they discovered their true identity. It will be no different for you. Nothing will make you more fearful than not knowing your own strength. You cannot be timid when it comes to going after your dream.

God needs you to believe in your purpose as if your life depends on it--because it does! Another reason I believe God does this is to show you that He is using you to start a fight. God wants to see how much you are willing to fight for the vision He planted inside of you. As you know, nothing in life comes easily. Failure is a part of success. It is the test you will have to take. Unfortunately, many people fail this test. They give up on themselves and God. They return to the safe, secure life they always knew, not knowing that success was on the other side of failure. If they only would have stayed in the fight long enough to get tired, then God would have stepped in and taken over when needed. God will fight with you, but you must stay in the fight until He shows up.

Failure is God's way of getting you to invite him into the fight. Sometimes we go into a fight in the name of God. We do like Moses and say, "God sent me!" However, we forget that not only did God send us, but He will fight alongside us. You get that small nugget? *God will not fight for you, but with you*. This is where many people lose heart. Like Moses, they want God to do all the fighting. No! God wants you right in the midst of the fight with Him. Therefore, He allows you to fail so that you can take up your cross and go to battle. Failure allows God to cultivate two things in you: faith and trust.

God doesn't always bless you with material things. Often God will bless you with an opportunity. It is what we do with the opportunity that really shows what we're capable of. Few people see the value of an opportunity. What is an opportunity, anyway? The root word of opportunity is "port," which means "access." The word access means to have permission to approach.

David would not have had access to the throne if God had not provided the opportunity. The fact he remained faithful as an unknown shepherd boy made it easier for God to choose him. He was anointed and was still left in the field. Opportunities are not always obvious. Many opportunities God will send your way will appear in the form of a problem. It will be something you have to fight to obtain. Opportunities come not to prove your strength, but to show the world God's ability. God wants to use your life as a testimony of His strength. However, if you try to depend on your own strength, you will not see God show up. I admit that waiting on God is difficult. It requires total trust and patience.

Remember when Moses went to Pharaoh the first couple of times and Pharaoh embarrassed him? Moses came back to God upset. He thought

God had let him down. God did allow Moses to fail. The Bible even said that God hardened Pharaoh's heart, so he would not let the people go. What seemed like a death sentence was in reality an opportunity. Moses initially rejected God's request because he saw it as a problem, not as an opportunity.

Opportunities are all around us. We miss them because they come with problems. Opportunity and problems are travel companions. When you see one, the other is never too far behind. Think about it. Every wonderful opportunity you ever had in life required you deal with some sort of problem. If you got a new job, it came with a problem. Maybe you had to move to another state. Maybe it meant working longer hours. Perhaps someone sold you a used car at a great price. But now you have to get car insurance and perform maintenance. Or say you just got approved for your first home. It's yours for the next thirty years. No more one-year leases! No more calling the leasing office and requesting the maintenance guy to come fix that water leak. God often calls us at the most inopportune times. It seems like when we are in our worst situations God comes and speaks a word to us. It is during these times we must have faith in ourselves. God wants our trust, not our faith. Now I hear you saying, "But the bible says, 'without faith it is impossible to please God'" (Hebrews 11:6). I tell people this is true, but faith is for you, not God. God wants you to have faith in the abilities and strengths He planted inside of you. I repeat, faith is for you, not God. You don't put your faith in a chair when you sit down. You pull the chair up and sit down. You had faith to sit down because you trusted the chair would support you. This is the same with God. The only way you can have faith in your abilities is to trust God, who provided you with the ability. Knowing this, you'll see failure in a different light. Failure is an opportunity to trust God, as well as an opportunity to grow your faith. Now reread that same scripture in the light of what I just said and see if it makes more sense:

*Without faith, it is impossible to please God!* Hebrews 11:6

Notice the comma? The "without faith" references not faith in God but yourself. The scripture never said without faith in God; God doesn't need our faith. He desires our trust. You can have faith in God all day long, but if you don't trust God, you will not accomplish the purpose God has given you. David had to learn this lesson like everyone else. David was willing to fight

Goliath. David trusted God, but he also had faith in his own ability. This made him a powerful weapon in God's hand. **David did not defeat Goliath; God defeated Goliath using David's faith.** David did not doubt himself nor God. Many times, we trust God, but we lack faith in ourselves. As a result, God cannot utilize us when we lack faith. It is the lack of faith that prevent us from taking the necessary risk to be successful. Remember, it was Jesus who said, *"Nothing is impossible for the one who believes."* Notice He never said "believe" or "have faith in God." He simply said, "the one who believes" or "the one who has faith." Did you catch that? He said nothing is impossible. Why? Because with trust in God, all things are possible. But you only attract God with trust in Him and faith in yourself. However, in order to activate your faith, you must learn to communicate it to others and create the most powerful force in the world: connections.

## Communicate Faith to Make Connections

*Draw near to God and God will draw near to you.*
James 4:8 NIV

On December 17, 2017, there was an enormous power outage in Atlanta, Georgia. And it wasn't just any power outage: It was a power outage at the world's busiest airport, Hartsfield Atlanta. Thousands of passengers, planes, and airline pilots were stuck on the tarmac for nearly six hours. The federal government was notified as local officials scrambled to fix the problem. The world watched with anticipation as the busiest airport came to a standstill. Some people feared the worst and thought maybe a terrorist group was responsible. It turned out it was just a regular power outage and the backup generator failed to power up. Everyone was relieved. Flights resumed, and business soon returned to normal. The incident was a perfect example of what happens when we lose connection: we become motionless and cease to function.

Although the power outage happened in Atlanta, it caused a ripple affect around the world. Nearly two thousand worldwide flights were canceled or delayed. The story was on every news station. As I listened to the news, I realized the importance of connections. The loss of electrical power not only shut down an airport, but it immobilized an entire industry. A loss of connection disabled power and stopped all movement. When you think about it, this is not only true for the airlines, but it is the way the world works. The world is built on connections. You and I exist because of a connection made in a woman's womb. Connections make life possible. Martin Luther King stated, *"We must all learn to live together as brothers or we will all perish together as fools. We are tied together in the single garment of destiny, caught in an inescapable network of mutuality. And whatever affects one directly affects all indirectly. For some strange reason I can never be what I ought to be until you are what you ought to be. This is the way God's universe is made; this is the way it is structured."* The world as we know it exists because of connections we call relationships.

Being able to connect is a big part of success. Another word for connections is relationships. You cannot be a success without being able to have great relationships, ones that make connections. We were created to be in relationships. Everything is connected and has a relationship with something else; nothing exists in isolation. Go ahead, think of one thing that doesn't need connection. I'll wait! If you find an answer e-mail me, but make sure you have an Internet connection first.

Success in today's world requires you to be able to connect or build relationships. In fact, we prosper or fail based largely on our relationships. The primary relationship that determines all other relationships is the one we have with ourselves. This relationship will determine our connections with our money, goals, family, friends, and God-given gifts.

We were each given a gift. However, the gift was created to work in conjunction with other people's gifts. No one succeeds alone. An author needs an editor and a publisher. An entertainer needs an audience, a promoter, a manager, and an agent. All of these things require connection.

It is difficult to make connections with others when you have no faith in who you are. When I have faith in myself, I make authentic connections with others. Security is no longer my concern. I become focused on building and creating. Look what God said when the people came together, used their unique gifts, and established strong connections:

*But the Lord came down to see the city and the tower the people were building. The Lord said, 'If as one people speaking the same language they have begun to do this, then nothing they plan to do will be impossible for them.'* Genesis 11:5-6

Amazing! God said nothing would be impossible for the people because they had faith in themselves to accomplish such an enormous task. Look what God had to do to stop them from building their dream:

*Come, let us go down and confuse their language so they will not understand each other. So the Lord scattered them from there over all the earth, and they stopped building the city.*
Genesis 11:7-8

Do you see what happened? The people's faith in themselves caused God to take action. God had to confuse their language to stop them from building. When they could not understand each other, they lost their faith and their connection. As a result, it affected their relationships. When their relationship failed, so did their mission. Now the people only trusted and connected with the people they could understand, a much smaller group. They lost faith in the  people with whom they could not connect. Faith requires connection and communication. Many people think of faith as simply believing something. Faith must be connected to something and communicated in a language that everyone can understand. In other words, I should be able to hear your faith in your actions. Perhaps you're remembering that the Bible says, *"Faith is the substance of things hoped for and the evidence of things not seen."* (Hebrews 11:1) Yes, this is the definition of faith, but not the practice of it. The practice of faith should manifest itself in our lives.   And don't miss the word evidence in that definition.

Nothing destroys faith more than not being able to communicate. Faith is how you communicate with your purpose. Faith is a language and doubt is a foreign language that your purpose doesn't understand. Your purpose only understands the language of faith. Your purpose will not answer to doubt, because it cannot understand it. This is the lesson from the Tower of Babel: Communication is the key to connection. Without connection, nothing gets done and nothing can grow. You are always communicating. There is no such thing as silence. You actions speak louder than words. *"But someone will say, "You have faith; I have deeds." Show me your faith without deeds, and I will show you my faith by my deeds."* James 2:18. When it comes to

God, everyone speaks two languages. You either speak faith or doubt. Yes, faith and doubt are languages, and God can only hear one. Which language are you speaking?

When doubt starts speaking to you, it causes faith to depart. Faith doesn't want to learn, nor does it know how to interpret the language of doubt. This is why failure is necessary. Failure causes either faith or doubt to speak loudly in your life. God introduces you to failure so you can learn to speak faith into your life. When you speak faith, you invite God into your life. When you speak doubt, you tell God you do not need His assistance.

If you read the Tower of Babel

scripture again, you will see that God came down and interrupted the people because they had faith. Because they had faith in the wrong thing, God interrupted their progress. Nonetheless, it certainly got God's attention. Faith gets God's attention. God introduces you to failure so you can attract His attention. Experiencing failure is the only way you will discover if you have faith or if you are just simply wishing. Don't run from failure; confront it and watch God move on your behalf.

David knew that if he had the faith to fight Goliath, God would fight alongside him. Listen to what he said right before he fought Goliath:

*Who is this uncircumcised Philistine that he should defy the armies of the living God?*
I Samuel 17:26

David summoned God with his faith. He had failed enough times to know not to be afraid of failure. He had seen God show up when he kept fighting. David had been in enough fights to know that God doesn't show up until the fight begins. If you run from the fight like Saul and the Israelites did, you will never see God come along and defeat your enemies. Notice that God did not intervene when Saul and the Israelites were hiding. God wanted someone to step into the fight with the Philistines. God birthed you to start a fight. You are already equipped to address a specific problem on this Earth. What is your fight? Maybe it is injustice, racism, abuse, hunger, poverty, or sickness. You will only know your purpose when you are willing to fight for it with everything you have.

**Listen to Your Problems; God Is Talking!**

The Bible is filled with great miracles. We often celebrate the miracles but miss the principles they teach. Every miracle in the Bible highlights how God uses unconventional methods to solve impossible problems. Problems are God's way of inviting us to get involved with issues bigger than ourselves. It is here that God shows us the power of even the smallest things. God separates the Red Sea with a staff. The massive walls of Jericho come down just with a loud shout. Moses confronts a king with just a word from God. Gideon defeats an entire army with just 300 men. Jesus uses a small kid to feed a multitude with five loaves and two fish. Problems are God's way of speaking to our faith. I wish I would have known this truth when I was going through the most challenging times in my life.

At the age of 43, I filed for bankruptcy. My car was repossessed, and I was on the verge of losing my home. It was clear that I had problems. I attempted multiple solutions. I prayed. I read books. I sought advice. I fell into the trap of doing what most people do when they face problems: I tried to solve my problem. I focused on the problem and not the lesson the problem was trying to teach me. You see, all my financial woes were a result of me trying to create a false image. I was trying to fit in and get approval from people who didn't even know me. I racked up student loan debt to get degrees. I wanted to be an intellectual so I could impress people with my knowledge. I bought a BMW I could not afford. I traveled and stayed in expensive hotels. The debt kept climbing, and I thought this debt alone was my problem. It wasn't. My problem was that I didn't think I was good enough. I was going out and buying things to improve my image and get approval. My real problem wasn't financial debt, it was spiritual hunger. Once I listened to my problem, I could use it to correct my problem. I discovered problems are guides. They lead you to the underlying cause. However, many people want the problem to go away. As a result, they ignore the lesson or try to cover it up.

Samuel anointed David as king, but he did not immediately take the throne. He had to wait until God moved him into the position. David's purpose showed up as a problem. *Hold up! Wait a minute!* Did you catch that truth? DAVID'S PURPOSE SHOWED UP AS A PROBLEM. David's life purpose depended on his willingness to face a giant problem in the form of Goliath. David defeated the problem and lived happily ever after. Wrong! You would think that after such an impressive victory and show of faith in God,

David would be set to take over the throne. Wait! Not so fast!

David had a lot to learn. He had to learn to trust God not just with his life but with the life of those who God entrusted to him. The bible tells us that David was forced out of the king's palace by Saul, but it was God who forced David out of the palace and into the wilderness.

The Bible stated that an evil spirit from the Lord harassed Saul. Saul tormented David and caused him to flee into the wilderness. It was there that David met a group of distressed and depressed men (1 Chronicles 12). Again, notice that God doesn't send David blessings, but problems. So, I want you to know each time you pray for a blessing, you are asking God for problems. Don't you dare put this book down now - if you do, we're going to have a problem.

# I Got 99 Problems, but My Heart Ain't One

*Guard your heart above all else, for it determines the course of your life.*
Proverbs 4:23 NLT

*"It takes real courage to allow yourself to feel pain."* Brene Brown

In 2004, I packed my books and my clothes in my truck and drove away from my newly-purchased home. I had only lived there for a couple of years. Now, I was leaving it for good. It was not my choice to leave. It was ordered by the court. My divorce was finalized, and I had to move out immediately. My ex-wife won the rights to the home. However, the house was still in my name. I was still responsible for the payments if she defaulted on the loan. I arrived at my new residence, a crowded apartment complex. I was moving from a three-bedroom, two-story home into a small one-bedroom apartment. My financial debt prevented me from buying any furniture, and I was angry at the world and at God. My mind wondered, "God, why would you let this happen to me" I felt betrayed. For the next couple of years, I lived alone. I vowed to never get into another relationship. God had me right where he wanted me; I was heartbroken.

I closed myself off from the world. I didn't want to feel anything. But I did let one feeling dominate my existence: self-pity. I started to feel sorry for myself. I wanted to be like the Tinman from *The Wizard of Oz*; I wanted to be heartless. It is interesting that when we talk about feelings we always mention the heart. Although the physical heart is not responsible for our emotions; it is our brain. Yet, we do have a spiritual heart. And just like the physical heart keeps our bodies alive, it is our spiritual hearts that keep us spiritually healthy. When we hurt spiritually life can be a pain. The heart is the first thing we cover up and hide once we are hurt. We subconsciously make a vow to never allow anyone to cause us pain in our hearts again. This is, however, a big mistake.

You have heard the saying, "A closed mouth never gets fed!" Well, *"A closed heart never gets led!"* A closed heart is one that is unavailable to God. When we close our heart, we become fearful and attempt to protect ourselves from hurt. As a result, we become afraid to step out in faith and take risks. You will never have success without taking risks. The first thing God does when He summons you is to deal with your heart. He must break down the walls around your heart so he can plant His desires there. A hard heart is equivalent to hard soil. Consider what Jesus said about a hard heart in the Parable of the Sower:

*That same day Jesus went out of the house and sat by the lake. Such large crowds gathered around him that he got into a boat and sat in it, while all the people stood on the shore. Then he told them many things in parables, saying: 'A farmer went out to sow his seed. As he was scattering the seed, some fell along the path, and the birds came and ate it up. Some fell on rocky places, where it did not have much soil. It sprang up quickly, because the soil was shallow. But when the sun came up, the plants were scorched, and they withered because they had no root. Other seeds fell among thorns, which grew up and choked the plants. Still, other seeds fell on good soil, where it produced a crop—a hundred, sixty or thirty times what was sown. Whoever has ears, let them hear.'*
Matthew 13:1-9

The soil in this parable is a metaphor for the heart. Do you see how Jesus contrasts the different types of soils? However, it is only the good soil that produces anything of value. What makes the soil good? It has been cultivated or broken up and made fertile. This is the only way that seeds can take root and produce fruit. Your heart can be likened to the soil; it must be broken (cultivated). I know you are saying to me, "But Kevin, I thought God wanted to heal my heart!" Well, God wants to use you to heal people. Therefore, He must heal you first. It is the only way you will be convinced that true healing is possible. You cannot truly love with a hard heart. A hard heart also prevents us from placing our trust in God.

A hurt person guards his heart from God and others. This is the natural thing to do when we have been hurt. When we get hurt in a relationship, we tell ourselves that we are done with looking for love. We vow to stay single or be extra selective in our future choices. The problem is, you can't guard your heart. When you shut down and protect yourself from people, you also hide your heart from God. God wants to use your heart to help people who are hurting. However, He has to get you to become vulnerable enough to hand your heart over to Him. Therefore, He must break the outer layer you have erected around your heart to protect yourself. Protecting yourself from pain is like carrying a false god with you. It becomes a security blanket. This is why God told the Israelites to remove their false gods before he moved them toward their true purpose. Israel carried false gods for security. It was their "just in case" backup plan. You know the plan you have "just in case" God doesn't come through for you. The person you keep dating until God brings the right one your way. The job you keep working until God blesses you with that winning lottery ticket. You know what I am talking about; the idol you are carrying around in your heart in the event God doesn't show up. This is what the bible means by putting away idols. Putting away idols means to surrender your heart to God.

The Israelites needed to put their complete trust in God. It is the same for you. God will not move you to your purpose until you allow Him to break the hard casing around your heart. This will make you vulnerable. I must admit that a vulnerable heart is uncomfortable, but it is the only way you will heal. Every Sunday, people go to the altar asking for healing, but they don't want to let go of the pain. The pain has become a hard shell protecting them from experiencing even deeper pain. As a result, God cannot get to the deep-rooted pain that is preventing you from being healed. In order to be healed, you must allow God to break the wall around your heart. You cannot heal from pain you are not willing to confront. So, when you ask for healing, don't be surprised if you feel heartbroken. A vulnerable, broken heart is a powerful tool in the hands of a mighty God.

God selected David to be king primarily because of his heart. David is a prime example what kind of heart attracts God! God told Samuel that David was a man after his own heart. God doesn't look for people with the biggest talent but those with the biggest heart. This is the heart that is not afraid to be hurt. It is a heart that is open and vulnerable, a heart available for intimacy.

Go through the Bible and you will see this pattern. God makes all his chosen people vulnerable before using them for His purpose. Moses was sent to the back side of the desert so that healing from his past could take place. Job was allowed to lose everything and have his heart broken before He allowed God into his pain. The Israelites had to stay in the wilderness and were broken before they started to pursue God's promise. *A broken heart is required before a healed heart can be acquired.* A hurt heart is a protected one. God knows that a hurt heart is a stubborn one. A hurt heart will not take risks. It will seek to be safe and comfortable, and God has no use for such a heart. Think back to the last time your heart was broken. What did you do? You enclosed yourself and started feeling sorry for yourself. You did not want to date again or eat, for that matter. Your family and friends could not reach you because you had closed yourself off from the world. You were vulnerable. Your heart was exposed and you were afraid to allow anyone near it, including God. However, this is the perfect time for God to transform you and begin the healing process. Now, I know some of you reading this are saying, "Well, it wasn't God who broke my heart but a person." While that may be true, God knew exactly what he was doing by allowing you into that relationship. **Sometimes God will allow you to have the bad thing before He brings the right thing along.**

Success requires that you take risks. You must get rid of your security blanket. Security has stopped many people from walking into their purpose, and it is still stopping many people today. We are taught security and safety very early in life. We grow up searching for security either in our jobs or other people. When we cannot find it in external places, we try to use our strength. At times, this may mean pretending we don't need love from others. We tell ourselves we are happy when we are truly yearning for acceptance. Admitting we need others makes us vulnerable, so we harden our hearts. It becomes tough for anyone to reach us on an intimate level, including God. When God comes looking for a person to do big, important things on Earth, He doesn't look for people with big titles, big degrees, or big positions. When God wants something done, He simply searches for a vulnerable heart. A vulnerable heart is available to be used by God. It is what qualifies you to be used by God. This is why forgiveness is such a big thing in God's sight, because it causes you to let go and make yourself available. Many people miss this small thing because they don't see how a lack of forgiveness is stopping them from hearing and seeing God. When we don't forgive, we make our hearts hard. This causes us to be very angry and judgmental. We become deaf and blind to signs from God and the opportunities that He provides us. We miss the opportunities that are right in front of our eyes. We close ourselves off to God and the world. You can never be successful that way. If you won't listen to me; hear what David has to say.

> Create in me a pure heart, O God, and renew a
> steadfast spirit within me. Psalm 51:10

Are you in a situation because of a stubborn, hard heart? If so, you must ask God to show you your heart. You may have some pain buried deep down in your heart that has you stuck in a dark place. I assure you that God will not allow you to move forward into your purpose with that type of heart. God moves your heart before He moves you into your destiny.

The people of Israel were still hurt from their slavery in Egypt, but they did not let God heal them from that pain. As a result, they became very afraid and sought to be safe from all risks and harms. This made them want someone else to bear the responsibility of keeping them safe. The people wanted to choose their own king, and they chose one who appeared fit for the part. They knew God wanted their hearts. They were not willing to give God their hearts because that would have made them vulnerable.

A king was far more controllable than God could ever be. They could manipulate a king and keep their hearts hidden. God did not want this for His people, but He allowed it to show them it was the wrong choice. When we think of kings, we think of strength. When God thinks of kings, He thinks of an available broken heart.

When selecting a king to replace Saul, God went looking for a vulnerable man. God needed someone whose heart was open and not guarded. I am sure David had reasons to guard his heart, but he kept an open heart, which allowed him to be vulnerable. David's heart is the type of heart that God seeks. An heart available to God is one that is vulnerable and not afraid of disappointment. However, this is the most difficult heart to find because of the inherent pain in the world. When we get hurt, it is natural for us to try and protect ourselves. We do this in a variety of ways. One of the most common ways we do this is by separating ourselves emotionally. We see the world as a dangerous place. As a result, we view people with caution and allow no one close to our hearts. We can never be healed this way. God will not allow you to heal in isolation. You must make your heart available to God. If not, you will begin to live an inauthentic life and your relationships will be forged. As a result, we find ourselves working for love and acceptance. Instead of trusting God, we fight Him.

## Wrestling with God

*That night Jacob got up and took his two wives, his two female servants and his eleven sons and crossed the ford of the Jabbok. After he had sent them across the stream, he sent over all his possessions. So, Jacob was left alone, and a man wrestled with him till daybreak. When the man saw that he could not overpower him, he touched the socket of Jacob's hip so that his hip was wrenched as he wrestled with the man. Then the man said, "Let me go, for it is daybreak."*

*But Jacob replied, "I will not let you go unless you bless me."*

*The man asked him, "What is your name?"*

*"Jacob," he answered.*

*Then the man said, "Your name will no longer be Jacob, but Israel, because you have struggled with God and with humans and have overcome."*
Genesis 22:32-22-28

I sat on my therapists' couch with my hands clenching my pants. My palms were sweating; I was nervous. The silence in the room was painful. Beads of sweat slid down my back as I tried to remain calm. Across from me sat an

African American male therapist. He was tall, had a low haircut, and very well dressed. He looked harmless, but so did other males who harmed me. All sort of thoughts ran through my head as he stared at me. The last time I was in a room alone with a male was when I was a teenager. *It was my high school track coach. He had invited me and some of the guys from the track team over for Bible study. He picked me up in his vehicle and drove me to his downtown apartment. Once we got inside I expected some of my teammates to be waiting but they were not. He told me the guys from the track team called and said they would not be able to make it. I entered his residence and he asked me to lie down; he wanted to stretch my muscles for the next track meet. I thought nothing of his request because he was an experienced track coach, as well as a pastor I thought I could trust. It never occurred to me that he might touch me inappropriately. I was laying on my back, stretched across his living room floor. I noticed he began to rub further up my leg as he discussed his upstairs neighbor. He began to tell me his upstairs neighbor was an attractive single woman who liked young boys. He began asking me if I ever had sex with a woman. The conversation made me uneasy. Just when I attempted to stand up he touched me in my midsection. I screamed and told him to take me home. I never told anyone. I stayed away from him for the rest of track season. When the season was over I quit the track team.*

Now here I was in a room with a man whom I had just met. The memory of my track coach sent me into a post traumatic trance. The therapist broke the silence with the question, "I make you uncomfortable, don't I? You are not comfortable around males?" At that very moment it felt like a presence entered the room. A cool breeze rushed across my face and I felt my spirit reenter my body. The heaviness was gone. My body no longer felt like a weight. It felt like it was one with my spirit. I was present for the first time in forever, and it felt strange. I could hear and feel my chest rise and fall. I remember thinking, *"I'm breathing. What is happening to me"* The therapist just looked at me. He was calm. It was if he knew what was taking place. Then he called my name, "Kevin!" At that very moment I answered, "Hello!" I stared at my hands and feet. I was back. I had been absent from my body for nearly 30 years and just like that I was back. We didn't talk much that day. I was given an appointment to come back the following week. Little did I know I was about to be in the fight of my life - with God.

My therapy session made me face my greatest fears. It made me remember things I thought I had forgotten. I learned something about myself each time I returned. I must admit it was a painful experience in the beginning. However, after a while I began looking forward to the sessions. My therapy sessions were my encounters with God. God had brought me face to face with my Jacob (false image). I had lived my whole life as Dee Dee, Officer McNeil, Detective McNeil, and Minister McNeil. But never as Kevin. I had created false images, so I could be accepted. Like Adam and Eve, I covered myself with titles and hid from God and the world. When the therapist called my name in the office that day I felt alive. Before then I was dead, but now, I had wrestled with God and lived.

Just like me, something happened to you!

Something happened to you! Something happened to you. I repeat this phrase because I want you to know, *I know something happened to you.* I know something happened to you and you know something happened to you; you can rest assure **GOD KNOWS SOMETHING HAPPENED TO YOU!**

God wants to wrestle your struggles away from you. But, like Jacob, you are holding onto them. Like Jacob, you are using material things to comfort you. Maybe you are using sex, alcohol, or drugs. Isolation may be your painkiller of choice. Whatever it is, God wants to wrestle it away from you so you can move forward. Esau represented Jacob's past. Jacob was attempting to run from his past. God forced him to confront it. It will be no different for you. God will force you to confront what you are *running* from before He allows you to *walk* in your purpose. Jacob wrestled God right before he went back to meet Esau. Esau represents all of Jacob's pain, fears, regrets, disappointments, and failures. He could not face those things until he got rid of his false image. It will be the same for you. The reason you keep losing battles is that you are fighting with a false image. God will only show up and help you fight when the real you show up. After you confront all these things, God will then address your expectations. The first struggle is how you see yourself. The second will be your attempt to control other people's perception of you.

We often live our lives based on other people's expectations. These expectations come from our parents, friends, or peers. Often our image becomes our security blanket. We try to protect it at all costs, even if it is detrimental to our success. I protected a faulty image of myself for 42 years. It took God that long to get me to put down my false idol: my image. Because I got my image from my family and friends I held it as sacred to me, even when it was hurting me. I felt I had to protect the shy little boy image to be accepted by family and friends. We gauge how successful we are by using other people's measuring tools. In fact, other people's expectations of us become the parameters with which we judge ourselves. When we set out to do something, we automatically think about what others might think of us. We do this subconsciously. Books are written, businesses started, churches formed because people were living up to someone else's expectation. We measure our worth by other people's expectations. Therefore, we feel like we have to be great or perfect in order to be loved.

We live in a world where everyone feels entitled to greatness. We are in the age of motivational speakers, mega-church pastors, and life coaches, where everyone is told that they are exceptional. Our e-mails are being flooded with messages on how to be the best in your business, the best looking of your friends on social media, or the most successful person in your circle. In today's society, average means boring. We look at Instagram and Facebook and see pictures of people flying first class, eating at the best restaurants, and worshipping at the biggest churches. It seems like everyone is living life to the fullest, while it seems like the rest of us are living an average life. We then feel depleted.

We may even get depressed because we feel we are missing out on life, although the representation that most people present on social media is far from their actual truth. We love to let people know we are not average. We want everyone to know we are different, special, and unique. As a result, we go out and try to make our lives extraordinary. We miss God by thinking that way, because God is not looking for an extraordinary person to change the world. He is just looking for an average person to help other average people live extraordinary lives. David was average in every stretch of the imagination. However, he was responsible. God would test David with small things before he gave him the throne. God starts small. We lose this insight because we can't imagine a big God doing little things. However, if you look through the Bible, you will see God loves the average. Moses, Abraham, Ruth, and Rahab were all average people who God uses in mighty ways. Jesus even chose twelve ordinary men to be his disciples. When God seeks change in the world, he doesn't go looking for the extraordinary. He looks for an ordinary person willing to do extraordinary things.

When we feel like we are special, we also feel like we are entitled. David fell under this spell when he was getting too old to fight in battle, and the men left him at home as they went off to fight a war. He felt like he had lost some power and needed a way to assert some of his authority. So, he slept with Bathsheba and had her husband killed to cover up his misdeed. Do you see what happened? Once David saw himself as extraordinary, he saw another man's life as merely ordinary and dispensable. If we are honest, the biggest thing holding us back is often our reputation. I must warn you this will be the first thing God comes after when pulling you into your purpose. The quickest way to summon God is to erect an idol. Look what God did to those who tried to protect their image.

## Job

Job had everything anyone one could ask for in life. He had a lovely family, riches, and good health. He was living a secure, stable life. However, if you read the story carefully, Job had an image to protect. When it was all taken away, Job found himself alone. His wife turned against him when he lost his security and his image. His friends scolded him and told him to repent of any wrongdoing. When Job lost all his security, he discovered a deeper trust and understanding in God. Why? God was not interested in his image. God wanted Job's heart. Job saw his life a measurement of God's presence. Because, like most of us, Job wanted assurance and tangible proof that God was with him. This does not require faith at all. Faith requires that we allow ourselves to be naked before God. We must not cover ourselves and hide behind false images. God cannot see us when we do and often has to call out to us, *"Where are you?"* When we chose to hold onto our false images, God has no choice but to let us wander lost. The Children of Israel learned this lesson the hard way.

## The Children of Israel

The Children of Israel learned this lesson when they were leaving Egypt (a place of security) and were heading to the wilderness (a place of insecurity). When we read about the Israelites enslaved in Egypt we pity them. We see them as helpless. We often miss the fact it was Israel's search for security that led them into bondage:

*Now there was a famine in the land—besides the previous famine in Abraham's time—and Isaac went to Abimelek king of the Philistines in Gerar. The LORD appeared to Isaac and said, "Do not go down to Egypt; live in the land where I tell you to live. Stay in this land for a while, and I will be with you and will bless you. For to you and your descendants I will give all these lands and will confirm the oath I swore to your father Abraham. I will make your descendants as numerous as the stars in the sky and will give them all these lands, and through your offspring all nations on earth will be blessed, because Abraham obeyed me and did everything I required of him, keeping my commands, my decrees and my instructions." So Isaac stayed in Gerar.*
Genesis 26:1-6

*"For thus says the LORD of hosts, the God of Israel: As my anger and my wrath were poured out on the inhabitants of Jerusalem, so my wrath will be poured out on you when you go to Egypt. You shall become an execration, a horror, a curse, and a taunt. You shall see this place no more. The LORD has said to you, O remnant of Judah, 'Do not go to Egypt.' Know for a certainty that I have warned you this day that you have gone astray at the cost of your lives.* Jeremiah 42

The Children of Israel were depressed and cried out to the Lord to free them from their bondage in Egypt. However, it was not just freedom they wanted; they wanted a different type of secure lifestyle. Life in Egypt was too hard and too unpredictable. They also wanted to be respected and have a better image of themselves.

*When the people saw that Moses was so long in coming down from the mountain, they gathered around Aaron and said, "Come, make us gods who will go before us. As for this fellow Moses who brought us up out of Egypt, we don't know what has happened to him."*

*Aaron answered them, "Take off the gold earrings that your wives, your sons and your daughters are wearing, and bring them to me." So all the people took off their earrings and brought them to Aaron. He took what they handed him and made it into an idol cast in the shape of a calf, fashioning it with a tool. Then they said, "These are your gods, Israel, who brought you up out of Egypt."*
Exodus 32:1-4 NIV

In the wilderness, they craved the security that Egypt brought them, even though they were enslaved. Many of us can identify with the

Israelites. We complain about our jobs, our relationships, and our situations. But each of the things we complain about brings us some level of security, so we remain in our comfort zone. When God calls us to freedom, He calls us into the world with no guarantees or warranties. He calls us into the unknown. This why we find it difficult to follow God, you must be willing to let go of everything, especially your securities. This is what it means to be a follower of Christ.

## The Disciples

Think about what Jesus asked the disciples to do. He asked them to leave not only their profession and follow him, but also their families. The disciples were secure as fishermen. Although fishing could be unpredictable, at least they had the security of knowing they had a job and skill set. Sound familiar? Then Jesus told them to drop everything and follow him to an unknown destination. Jesus did not have anything material to promise them for their troubles. He asked them to become insecure so that they could place their faith in God. Can you imagine as a disciple going home to tell your wife that you are going to quit your job to follow a carpenter from Galilee across the countryside to teach parables? This is what

Jesus required his disciples to do. However, Jesus was not asking them to do something he was not prepared to do himself.

## Jesus

Jesus is the ultimate insecure person in the scriptures. He attaches himself to nothing. He tells his followers to drop everything to follow him, and even tells one man desiring to follow him that "Foxes have holes, and birds of the air have nests, but the Son of Man has nowhere to lay his head." Jesus lives a life of insecurity. He does not allow anything to control Him. As a result, He is fully in control. Nothing drives home this truth more than the crucifixion where Jesus gives up his life so that others can follow his example of freedom. The lesson Jesus attempts to teach us is that freedom comes from detachment. He even asks, *"What will it profit a man to gain the whole world but forfeit his soul?"* The soul does not need security. This is a selfish endeavor. When we find ourselves afraid, it is because we fear losing something. We go into panic mode and put all our efforts into maintaining a sense of security just to lose our souls in the process. This brings us to David. David sought to be ordinary. He did not seek a life of wealth or security. David was not concerned about his image and God elevated him. David's life would be a valuable lesson to all of us who want to be in proper standing with God. Let go of your image so God can reveal your identity. You will never walk in purpose until you know your identity.

David had no image to protect. It is why God could easily anoint him King. What image are you protecting that is preventing God from promoting you to the next level?

## Your Call Might Not Match Your Situation

*Then Samuel took the horn of oil and anointed him in the midst of his brothers. And the Spirit of the Lord rushed upon David from that day forward.* 1 Samuel 16:13

Are you looking at your current situation and wondering if you will ever be successful? It is easy to get depressed looking at our current situations. We often doubt God is with us during the tough times. It seems like it is when we are in our worst situations that God comes and speaks to us. It is because of this fact, many people find it difficult to believe God is summoning. God called Abraham to be a father of many nations when his wife was barren. He called Moses to be a leader for justice while he was a fugitive. He called Gideon to be a champion when he was being a coward, hiding from the enemy. And He called David to be a king while he was still just a shepherd boy. Why? God wanted to see how they would handle their responsibilities in their current situations. It is the same for you. If you are irresponsible in your current situation you will also be irresponsible when your situation improves. However, many people try to wait until their situation improves before they do. They use their situation as proof God is active in their lives. Many pastors and prophets even encourage people to pray for their situations to change. God doesn't want to change your situation. God wants to change you, so you will be empowered to change your own situation. God changes people, not situations. Stop praying for God to change your situation. Ask God to change you. Your life is the gift God entrusted to you. If you are not responsible with your life, why would you be responsible with anything God gives you? You will never improve above your ability to be responsible with whatever you are given.

*One who is faithful in a little is also faithful in*

*much, and one who is dishonest in a little is also dishonest in much.* (Luke 16:10)

I put this principle into action once I learned it. I became more responsible in my health, finances, time, and thoughts. After several months, I noticed a momentous change in my routine. I went to bed earlier and woke up sooner. My exercise routine increased to three times a week. I no longer spent money on frivolous things. In short, when I changed, so did my situations. I was proud of myself and was tempted to post my progress all over social media. But I realized God was not done with me. Nature had taught me everything God prepares is hidden until it is ready to be revealed. I decided to continue on my journey in obscurity.

# Stay Hidden; God Will Find You!

*Jesus said to them, 'Have you never read in the Scriptures? The stone the builders rejected has become the cornerstone; the Lord has done this, and it is marvelous in our eyes.*
Matthew 21:42 NIV

High school was not my favorite time. My peers teased me and called me Captain Caveman (a cartoon character). Okay, you can stop laughing now. I know you just googled Captain Caveman. In all honesty I did look like him a little bit. I stood five foot and three inches. My head was big, and I wore a size eleven shoe. I was generally quiet, and when I did speak people said I was difficult to understand. They said I sounded like a caveman. My teenage years were depressing. I rarely smiled. It wasn't because people made fun of me; I never smiled because my teeth were in horrible condition. Growing up I never went to the dentist. My mom could not afford it.  None of these things stopped me from having the same desires as other boys my age. I loved sports, food, and girls. But no girl wanted to be near me. So, when it came time for my senior prom I was surprised I had a date.

In truth, it really wasn't a date, it was more like me giving her a ride to the prom. I didn't know at the time, but I was basically the world's first Uber driver. The girl agreed to go with me because she was mad at her boyfriend. She wanted to attend the prom so she could hang out with her friends. She made it clear to me there would be no extracurricular activities. I was instructed to just smile and pretend. I was basically her escort and driver. I didn't even have access to a car. We had to use her mother's Chevy Beretta. We parked the vehicle. She walked in front of me as I trailed behind. It was like I didn't even exist. Nonetheless, I was happy. At least I could say I was invited to go to the prom. Rejection never feels good, but I think it was good for me. This rejection led to my realization that I simply did not belong in Memphis. As a result, I decided to run away from home and join the military. I did not know it at the time, but God was hiding me. Sometimes God will use rejection to keep you from being common. God uses uncommon people to handle uncommon problems.

I was initially turned down by the military. The doctor told me I had bad feet and he could not sign off on my physical. I literally had to beg the doctor to let me into the military. I lied and told him it was a lifelong dream of mine. I was turned down for college due to my low GPA. I had to wait and go to a community college and take basic courses before I could pursue my degrees. Even as a police officer, I was recommended for termination within two weeks after graduating the academy. I was placed with a training officer whom I felt treated people unfairly. She thought I was too nice a person to be a police officer. She wanted to see more aggression from me, but that wasn't my personality. Thankfully, the training officer who recommended me for termination got sick the next day and did not turn in the paperwork. She was out for the next week, while I was assigned to another training officer who thought I was a great officer. When things like this happen, we often think it is a sign to choose something different or give up. However, I have learned that God hides you from people, so He can develop you. Like everyone God chooses in the bible, rejection is par for the course. Moses is initially rejected by the elders. Joseph is rejected by his family. Jesus is rejected by his peers and community. David is rejected by his own father and brothers. Why does God use rejection to prepare us? The word reject comes from the Latin word *rejicere*, which means *"to throw back."* In other words God places you in a holding pattern until you develop. If you are known prematurely, you may not be ready for the pressures of success. People rejected me because I was different. However, God used rejection to cover me and hide me as He developed me into the person He wanted. Rejection made me feel like I didn't belong. If forced me to hide. As a result, I flew under the radar. When people don't see you as valuable, they pay little attention. Premature attention can distort the growth and maturation process. Can you imagine digging up a diamond prematurely or a child being born way too early? God uses processes to develop us. It is why the wilderness is necessary. The wilderness is where God separates us and begins developing us for our purpose. It is where character-building and faith development occurs.

Like a precious diamond, God hides and prepares those He intends to use. Moses was hidden in the palace, David was hidden in the field, and Jesus was hidden in a manger. Why is this so significant? Let's look at nature for our answer. Have you ever noticed that things of value are hidden and take time to develop? For instance, diamonds and gold are hidden deep within the earth and are formed by pressure.

We don't read about David until halfway through the Old Testament. He was discovered just like all of God's chosen vessels: during a time of turmoil. David never asked to be king. He never planned for it or tried to place himself in a position to be king. He just was faithful with his current role. God used his current assignment to shape and mold him. When he was ready, God sent for him. You get that nugget! **God came looking for David.**

Every situation you have ever experienced is just God preparing you for your purpose. Nature teaches us that everything of value is hidden and takes time to form. You are no different. God uses every situation to teach us something. He does this to prepare us for our next position. Learning always proceeds promotion. Many people want to be promoted while remaining the same. The purpose of the lesson is growth. When you grow, you go. Like me, most people miss the lesson due to looking at their current situation. Stop complaining about where God plants you. Instead ask God what lessons are to be learned.

The lesson always takes place in your current position. I had to learn to be faithful in my position as a detective. For years, I complained about my position and did not learn to be faithful to the process. God would not release me because

I was too busy complaining. My complaining drowned out God's voice. When I stop complaining I could hear more clearly. As a result, I became more concerned about the welfare of my victims rather than the status of my cases. I discovered my assignment was not to place people in jail, but to release them from the effects of abuse. As I began to apply this principle, I no longer complained. Like David, God had me in training. We have no reason to believe that David ever complained about his role as a shepherd. David used his current condition to learn about God's faithfulness. David worshipped God even when it was not convenient to do so. Instead of complaining, he sought God for help. He then waited for God to move on his behalf. Because David knew how to stay hidden until God was ready for him, God fully developed him for the position of king. Are you allowing God to prepare you? Are you more concerned about position than you are preparation? King Saul is a fitting example on what happens when we fill positions without God's preparation. King Saul was thrust into a position he was not prepared to uphold. Notice that Saul was never prepared by God but was carnally picked to be king.

*He brought the tribe of Benjamin nearby its clans, and the clan of Matrites was taken by lot, and*

*Saul, the son of Kish, was taken by lot. But when they sought him, he could not be found, so they inquired again of the Lord, 'Is there a man still to come?' And the Lord said, 'Behold, he has hidden among the baggage.' Then they ran and took him from there.*

The people wanted Saul to be king because he looked like one. Saul did not want to be king, and he hid for a reason known best to himself. David allowed God to hide him. Saul hid because he was prideful and considered himself inadequate. Now, I know some people would ask, "I thought pride is thinking you are too much, not too little!" No, thinking you are too big is a cover up. Most people who think too highly of themselves are hiding their feelings of not being enough. Being prideful means that you do not think you are enough. This is pride in God's eye. When we tell God He created us as inadequate, we are essentially telling God that he must have made a mistake. So, when Saul was chosen as a king, his pride did not allow him to take the position because he thought he was inadequate. Many people mistake feelings of inadequacy for humility. However, it is false humility. If God created you, He wants you on Earth for a purpose. Who are you to tell God that you are not enough? Don't you think that is pride? Many of us are afraid like Saul because we know we will have to be prepared and be in a constant state of preparation to be successful. This means God will have to take us through stages where we will be uncomfortable. This is the stage where our vulnerable hearts get used by God to bring change into the world. Contrary to what we are being taught in church, this does not happen overnight and can take time. Many of us want to be successful, but we want instant success. We do not want to allow God to form us. We are told that God will do all the work and all we have to do is show up. We are disappointed to learn that this is not how God operates. If you don't believe me, look at the life of David. David had to work hard before ascending to the throne, even after he was anointed king 17 years earlier. He was protected and hidden by God. But he was also being formed with hard decisions and difficult tasks. Many of us seek to be used by God so we can receive all the benefits of being chosen. David shows us that calling comes with a price, a price no one else will never see or understand. There are reasons some people never make it to their promised land. I believe that not being hidden and not allowing God to shape and form us is one of the main reasons we fail to fulfil our purpose. Our purpose revels itself in God's hiding place.

God hides everyone He uses for His

purposes. Israelites were hidden in the wilderness while God prepared them for the Promised Land. However, while in the wilderness they cried out and complained. At one point, they even wanted to return to the enslaved lifestyle back in Egypt. Do you see that? They considered slavery better than being hidden in obscurity and formed by God. Wait! Before you judge, what are you holding back that has made it difficult for God to prepare you for the next level? Are you remaining in a job, relationship, or mindset because it is too painful to finally move forward? What is stopping you from letting God work on you? Are you afraid that God will take certain things away from you and place you in a desolate place? Be honest with your answers.

## Sweat the Small Stuff

You have heard people say, "Don't sweat the small stuff." However, I am telling you that you must sweat the small stuff. It is the small stuff that makes the difference between success and failure. Successful people are this way because they made the insignificant things have significance. Remember, all massive things start off small, and that includes failure. Look at someone whose life is in turmoil and more than likely it did not happen overnight. The weight gain, heart attack, bad habits, and financial trouble did not just happen overnight. The big problem came from a lot of small unresolved problems. The small decisions we make every day get us into big trouble. Trouble rarely just happens, particularly trouble we caused ourselves. Think of some of the most successful people in the world and you will find that they capitalized on something small. Businesses like Chick-fil-A and Apple focused on small details, and it made their companies huge successes over time. Truett Cathy wanted the best chicken sandwich in the industry, but he focused on customer service. Now people not only go to Chick-fil-A for the delicious food, but also the wonderful smile they receive at the counter. Similarly, Steve Jobs made the small things important, which made his computer company stand out. He wanted his company's machines to have a clean and neat appearance. Something like the visual appearance of the company logo may be small to some people, but not to Jobs. He was willing to be different and spend tons of money on small details. Ignoring the small things will lead to big problems in the future. You must be willing to sacrifice what others may consider small if you wish to qualify for big responsibilities. David knew this principle well.

*And he said, 'There remains yet the youngest, and behold, he is tending the sheep.'*
1 Samuel 16:11

David gave attention to small things and it showed. When one of his sheep went missing, he put all his efforts into finding it. He could have easily said, "Hey, it's just one sheep. What is one out of a whole herd? I will protect the others. Losing one sheep isn't that bad." No, David put his life on the line for one sheep. Jesus even uses a parable about lost sheep to make this point. *"Suppose one of you has a hundred sheep and loses one of them. Doesn't he leave the ninety-nine in the open country and go after the lost sheep until he finds it?"* Jesus uses sheep because the job of a shepherd of sheep was reserved for a servant. If a family had enough money to have sheep and cattle they would hire a servant as their caretaker. So, David wasn't even considered family. Yet, God chose him to be king. Why? He was man after God's own heart, a heart that loved what others despised. The point Jesus was making is you're not qualified to handle big responsibilities until you develop a heart to look after what others consider insignificant. You cannot wait to be given something big; you must use whatever is currently in your hand.

## Use What Is in Your Hand

*And David strapped his sword over his armor, and he tried in vain to go, for he had not tested them. Then David said to Saul, 'I cannot go with these, for I have not tested them.' So David put them off. Then he took his staff in his hand and chose five smooth stones from the brook and put them in his shepherd's pouch. His sling was in his hand, and he approached the Philistine. 1 Samuel 17:39-40*

Saul and the people of Israel saw Goliath as a huge problem. Their eyes were fixated on his height and large weapons. As a result, they saw themselves as inadequate. Fear gripped their hearts as they compared their weapons to Goliath's. The king Israel had chosen for themselves was afraid to do the very thing he was hired to do: defend the nation with his life. Then along comes a small shepherd boy on a food delivery errand to his brothers. Look what they said about David when he showed up.

*When Eliab, David's oldest brother, heard him speaking with the men, he burned with anger at him and asked, "Why have you come down here? And with whom did you leave those few sheep in the wilderness?*

*I know how conceited you are and how wicked your heart is; you came down only to watch the battle."* 1 Samuel 17:28 NIV

Wow! You see what was said about David. He was called all sorts of names but it did not deter his belief in himself or God. David was seen as a weak Shepard boy but he was accompanied by a strong God; a god Israel could not see because they were relying on their own strength.

Don't make the same mistake as Israel. Acknowledge your God. First, God is with you. Secondly, God did not leave you empty-handed. You have something in your arsenal right now to defeat whatever problems you are facing. When David went to fight Goliath, he was only armed with a staff. Saul attempted to give David his armor, but he rejected it, for it had not been tested. David used his staff to retrieve five stones from the brook. Do you see that? David used what God had already given him. **God is not interested in giving you anything else until you use what you already have effectively.** Often, God will give you something small and see how responsible you will be with it.

Even Samuel, the prophet of Israel, missed this valuable point. He believed God would choose someone who looked similar to Saul. God allowed Saul to be king because the people of Israel wanted a  big, like all their surrounding nations.

Why didn't God just tell Samuel to go and anoint Jesse's son, David? It would have been easier. Samuel had to observe all of Jesse's sons. He was prepared to anoint one based on appearance alone, but God rejected all seven other sons. I believe God wanted to teach Samuel a lesson, one we can benefit from too. In fact, we hear God say, "God does not see as man sees." God looks for small details. But, like Samuel, most people look for great evidence. While we look for God in the big things, God is watching how we handle those small things.

Do you remember how David came to fight Goliath? David did not just stumble into a fight, nor did he go looking for a fight. David came upon the biggest opportunity of his life because he accepted a small task. His father tasked him with taking something to his brothers to eat.

*And Jesse said to David, his son, 'Take for your brothers an ephah of this parched grain, and theses ten loaves, and carry them quickly to the camp to your brothers. Also, take these ten kinds of cheese to the commander of their thousand. See if your brothers are well, and bring some token from them.'* 1 Samuel 17:17-18

Are you kidding me? Can you imagine being David? You have already been anointed king in front of everyone, and they still ask you to do nominal shepherding work. David could have gotten angry and refused to do such a menial task. He could have said, "I am God's anointed. I don't serve other people. I only answer to God!" but he did not take that position. Humbly accepting that small task eventually set him up for the biggest opportunity of his life. You see, God had already made the big change, but David had to take the small steps. Many people fail at this point. They only see God in the big things. Remember that it was a still, small voice that Elijah heard from God. Being able to recognize the small things and be responsible for them is big in God's sight.

*"The journey of a thousand miles begins with one step."* Lao Tzu

## You Already Have What It Takes!

When I first started my public speaking career, it was only to a handful of people, and I had to travel miles to get to my destination. Often, I did not have the gas money to travel to my destinations. I had to take days off of work to speak. I was not getting a paycheck nor recognition. God wanted to see how I would value the gift. Would I be willing to make sacrifices? We must have faith despite what our circumstances look like. David had a king in him even when it looked like he was going to spend his life as a shepherd boy. Oprah was a billionaire before the world ever knew her name. Author J. K. Rowling was a best-selling author before she sold even one book. It took the willingness to sacrifice and use their gifts in the world before the world recognized their gifts. Initially, you must pay for your gift before your gift starts paying you. So, this is what I will say to you: Stop complaining. Stop waiting. Stop looking. Use what you already have in your hand.

Let's pause right now and evaluate what you currently have in your hand. Let's take your job, for example. Are you complaining about going to work every day? Do you do just the bare minimum while there? Are you waiting to get paid and retire?

**TIME OUT**

Before we can move forward, let's look at how God measures one of your most valuable assets—your time. Let's take the average day. Everyone has twenty-four hours. It is true whether you are poor or rich. It's how you use those twenty-four hours that's important. Now, this is the first thing you must examine for yourself. How you use your time is one of the biggest things people overlook. Why? Because most people see it as something of little importance, especially when they are young. Time usually grabs our attention as we age.

Now, I hate using the phrase "waiting on God," because most people think that means just sitting by idly doing nothing. They believe that if they pray hard and long enough, God will grant their requests. I prefer the phrase "working with God." This means to get up every morning and use your time wisely toward what you believe God is calling you to accomplish on the Earth.

David did not spend his time daydreaming. We have the psalms to prove he was busy with his time. When you trust God, you trust his timing. It means that you work hard and allow God to process you. You do not get anxious or overwhelmed when things are not going the way you hoped. The Bible has so many examples of people who did not wait for God's timing. Abraham couldn't wait for God's timing and had Ismael. Moses got impatient with God and struck a rock when God informed him to speak to it. Saul could not wait for God's timing and made a forbidden sacrifice to the Lord. Even David disregarded God's timing when he impregnated Bathsheba and had her husband killed. Look what the prophet Nathan told David: *"I anointed you king over Israel, and I delivered you from the hand of Saul. I gave your master's house to you, and your master's wives into your arms. I gave you all of Israel and Judah. AND IF ALL OF THESE HAD BEEN TOO LITTLE I WOULD HAVE PROVIDED YOU EVEN MORE."* Did you hear that? David got impatient and started looking at his situation. As a result, he tried to change it himself to make himself happy. If we're not careful, we will try to rush God's timing and not be thoroughly prepared. Nature teaches us this fact. An oak tree takes years to grow so it can take on enormous storms. A diamond must endure heat and pressure before it can obtain its value. Babies develop in the womb for months. In the same way, you must allow God to process you into your purpose. How do you do this effectively? Use your time wisely.

## Small Ideas Need Big, Courageous Leaders

Two of my favorite television shows happen to be on Food Network and Home and Garden Television (HGTV). I know that is sort of weird for a male former police officer. However, I love the leadership principles these two shows demonstrate. Another show I love is on the Food Network; a cooking show called *Chopped*. It consists of four random chefs competing for prize money. The twist is they must take unusual ingredients and make a meal with them that the judges will taste. For example, the chefs may be given chicken gizzards, potato chips, and Junior Mints, and they have to make a meal that could be served in a restaurant. The judges are world-class chefs themselves, so it makes the competition even more challenging. If that were not enough, they are only given a limited time to make the meal. There are usually three rounds: an appetizer, entrée, and dessert round. Each round is judged and the chef with the least appealing dish gets chopped. After watching a number of episodes, I could guess who would win before the competition was over. How? Before the competition begins, the host asks each chef what they planned to do if they won the money. The person who mentioned they had a vision to take the prize money and create something almost always won. Why? They had a vision of where they were going. All the cooks were given the same ingredients but it was the person who knew how to direct (lead) those ingredients that won. Having a vision showed great leadership ability. In order to be a great cook, you must lead well. You must take ingredients with different qualities and make them work well together. It is the same formula for great leadership. Managers require good people and great tools to make things work effectively. Leaders can take what they are given and make it work.

The other show I like is *Flip This House*. This show also teaches a great leadership principle: True value exists on the inside. The show starts off with investors looking to get a competitive price on a foreclosed or unwanted home. They inspect the outside and try to determine whether to remodel the house and place it on the market. This type of investment can be tricky, because the buyers don't know what they are really getting until they get inside. The outside may look good, but it's the inside that will determine how much money they must really invest into the house. After purchasing the house, they must go inside the walls and look at the structure. It is at this point they run into most of their problems. When they remove the coverings, the true story emerges.

The wiring may be faulty or the plumbing inoperable. At this point, they can complain or take what they have and fix it. Leadership is much the same way. You won't understand the nature of the problem until you get really invested in the problem. Most people try to handle problems from a distance. However, to be a leader, you must be courageous enough to take on any challenges placed before you. Who knew you could learn leadership principles from cooking and home improvement shows? I guess John Maxwell was right when he said, *"Everything rises and falls on leadership."*

# Follow the Leader

*"Come, follow me," Jesus said, "and I will send you out to fish for people."*
Matthew 4:19 NIV

Why did Jesus choose fishermen to be disciples? I have asked this question many times. Fishermen want to catch fish. The best way to get a fisherman's attention is to show him how to catch fish. Now, like anything else, fishermen are willing to listen to other fishermen about fishing, but rarely would they listen to someone who has never fished – they trust their fellow experts. So how does a carpenter get a group of fishermen to follow him to an unknown destination? He meets them where they are and leads them to a prosperous place. Fishermen make great leaders because they must use a team to succeed. In biblical times fishermen had to be skillful with nets. They had to know how to cast them, clean them, and repair them. They had to know how to work with nets, or *they had to be able to net-work.* If you do not have great leaderships skills, it will be nearly impossible to lead a team. The Bible shows that before God uses someone, they have to go to leadership training. No one gets a pass. You must be able to lead well if you are going to be successful. It won't matter how talented you are if you have no leadership skills. Leadership skills determine how far your dreams can go. I have witnessed people with extraordinary talent and knowledge who struggled to be successful. It wasn't because they didn't have what it took to be successful. They were poor leaders. Have you ever asked yourself why a certain talented athlete or entertainer is no longer around? You envied their skills, now who knows where they are anymore. On the other hand, you see people like Jay Z, Peyton Manning, or Sean Combs reach elevated levels of success. Why? They became great leaders. If you do not lead well, you will not do well. No one wants to follow or listen to a poor leader.

Jesus told his disciples to follow him and He would make them fishers of men. Jesus was telling his disciples he would make them into leaders. A successful fisher required great skill and strength. It require pulling stubborn fish into a boat.Fishermen used bait and lured fish into their nets. Once they had the fish they then forced them into the boat. In other words, the fish had no choice but to go with the fishermen. You cannot lead people like you catch fish. People are more stubborn than fish. If you ever been fishing, you probably just shouted *Amen!* Jesus was not looking for followers; Jesus was looking for leaders.

Jesus came onto the boat and told the disciples to sail out deeper. When they did so, the fish willingly jumped into their nets. Again, as I mentioned earlier, we pay attention to the miracle but miss the principle to be learned. Leadership and blessings go hand-in-hand. We ask for more things when we are poor leaders of the things we already possess. We want more money but are drowning in debt. We want to own a business while despising our current job. We want a bigger home while we don't clean our current apartments. How are you leading what you currently have? Jesus was teaching the disciples that you must be a great leader before God can bless you the way He truly desires. Another lesson Jesus teaches is that we must be willing to take risks. Leaders must leave their comfort zones and convince others to travel with them. Jesus got into the boat with the men he wanted to lead. Jesus immersed himself in the culture he sought to change. Before getting people to follow them into the unknown, leaders must also be willing to go into dangerous territory. David did all these things before he even became king. The Bible said David led men no one considered worthy. Look at what the Bible says in 1 Samuel 2:22: *"All those who were in distress or in debt or discontented gathered around him, and he became their commander. About four hundred men were with him."* David went from being a shepherd, leading simple sheep, to being commander over a bunch of rejects. You see the progression? His task never got easier. He had to become a leader in his current situation before being promoted to a higher position.

## Are You a Manager or Leader?

Some people will say they managed an account or a team of people. They think this automatically makes them a leader. Just because you manage well doesn't mean you lead well. Others say, well, I manage my house well or I am great at managing my finances. This is also not a sign of effective leadership. In order to be a leader, you must be able to cause something to grow. If I gave you five dollars, managing it would be to place it in the bank. Leading the five dollars would be investing it in something that would double its value. For instance, if I ordered a John Maxwell leadership book from Amazon, I would be adding more value to the five dollars. Reading the leadership book would add more value to me, the possessor of any future earnings. Leaders not only make themselves better, they increase the value of anything in their charge.

If you don't want a lot of responsibility then, yes, being a manager may be your thing. Managers are good at keeping the status quo. However, when it comes to problem solving, managers fall short. Many organizations make the mistake of hiring managers instead of leaders. Their organizations run smoothly until a problem occurs. Managers are great at keeping things operating, but effective problem-solving requires actual leadership.

God will provide you with challenges to improve your leadership skills. We often run from challenges or complain when they show up in our lives. Before David fought Goliath, he had many challenges. One, he had to be okay with not being accepted by the masses. Saul never overcame this challenge. He wanted to be accepted and loved by everyone. Acceptance is a challenge for most people. The need to feel accepted is what causes some people to join sororities, fraternities, social media, and churches. Some people even join gangs to find acceptance. Acceptance begins within yourself. It is difficult for God to use you effectively if you place all your emphasis on what people think about you. **Leaders Are Focused on**

**improving others;  not on what others think of them.**

David had to learn to fight on behalf of others. He had to face threats to his father's flock of sheep. This is the true essence of leadership. You cannot be a leader if you are not willing to fight on behalf of others. Another major flaw of Saul is that he was trying to fight on his own behalf and not for the people. David fought Goliath on behalf of God and the people. You must keep in mind that God wants you to fight for His glory, not yours. Listen to what David said before he fought Goliath: "And David said to the men who stood by Him, "'What shall be done for the man who kills this Philistine and takes away the reproach from Israel? For who is this uncircumcised Philistine, that he should defy the armies of the living God?'" (1 Samuel 17:26-27) Do you see how David saw the problem? Instead of seeing Goliath as just a problem, he saw him as an issue that was stopping God's people from being successful.

# Nothing Big Ever Comes from a Small Mind

*As a man thinketh in his heart, so is he.*
Proverbs 23:7

When we think small, we are always searching for something to make us feel better. Small minds seek pleasure. Chasing pleasure always leads to a never-ending road. We use the word happiness instead of pleasure, but it is actually pleasure we seek. Happiness is just an enjoyable way of saying "I want to feel good." Now, I know you are asking what is wrong with being happy and feeling good? Nothing! It is just that it cannot solely be what you should be pursuing. What God is asking you to do will be difficult and challenging at times. If all you want to do is to become happy, you will be discouraged and never finish the journey. David was anointed king long before he took the throne. However, look at all the things he had to endure in between being anointed and being king. If he were seeking pleasure, he would have told God, "Never mind, God, I think I like this shepherd boy thing. It is not that bad after all." This is what many of us do when we seek God for pleasure. We expect that when we start doing what God wants us to do that life will get easier. When it doesn't, we get angry or disappointed. We then decide to give up. The majority of times it is because we are thinking too small. God has something way bigger in store for our lives. However, what God has for us requires us to be prepared. Remember, the Bible says, *"God will not put more on you than you can bear."* So, the hardships come as a way to prepare you for the big thing God has prepared for you. Pleasure is not a bad thing in itself, but it fades. If you simply seek pleasure, you will never accomplish anything of significance. Walking with God is a great experience, but it has its challenges and disappointments. The challenges and disappointments only exist because we are thinking too small. Even small problems are big for people with small minds. Small-minded people love easy things and feeling comfortable.

A big God cannot use a small mind. Although we are talking about small things to make big changes in your life, there are things that cannot remain small. You cannot have small faith or courage. The reason I stayed in a job where I was not appreciated for 20 years was not because of what others thought of me; it was because I thought small of myself. You will never outgrow your mindset. Your mindset is a container that determines your growth. I once heard that if you remove a baby shark from the ocean and place it in a fish tank, it will never outgrow the tank. However, take that same shark and put it in the ocean, and it will grow to its full capacity. Your mindset works similarly. God will not place big ideas in a small mind. Jesus said it this way: *"No one puts new wine into old wineskins. If he does, the wine will burst the skins, and the wine is destroyed, and so are the skins. But new wine is for fresh wineskins."* Mark 2:22 ESV

Think about Moses when God came to him with his mission. God especially chose him for this task, but Moses thought so little of himself that he rejected God's offer to live out his purpose. This is what happens when you think too little of yourself: you reject God. Remember, Moses was born to liberate Israel. God had saved him for this purpose. However, Moses could not understand how God worked. God did not abide by cultural norms. Moses was an unknown murderer on the run. He did not grow up in bondage like his fellow countrymen and their leaders. I am sure they thought their leader would come from their ranks, but God broke rank and chose Moses. Similarly, David was chosen to be king. Many of us have been conditioned to believe that God goes by our rules and standards. We go to seminary to become big-name pastors and God uses an enthusiastic guy like Joel Osteen, who never stepped foot in a seminary, to lead the largest church in America. He uses a comedian like Steve Harvey and a filmmaker like Tyler Perry to send life-changing messages to the masses. He uses twelve ordinary men to turn the world upside down and a carpenter from Galilee to change history. We often miss God because we think we need to do something big to be used by God. We think we need a degree, a special connection, or to come from a well-off family to be in God's good graces.

You need to know that God anointed you to fulfil a purpose on Earth! You will never be happy until you achieve that goal. You have a calling in your life. You were born for a purpose. You will never discover it if you keep focusing on your current situation. I walked away from a secure career with no money and no health insurance. This was not because of my situation; it was because I knew I had a call to pursue. I did small things that led to me leaving. The first thing I did was acknowledge that I had a calling. **Go ahead and do that now**. Admit that you have a calling. Do this every day when you wake up. I assure you that it is a small thing, but it is a powerful step. Most people fail because they do not think they have anything to give to the world. It is not because they don't have talent; it is because they perceive they have no value. God cannot use you if you think this way. The actual definition of pride is not thinking you are too much but thinking that you are not enough. God will not use anyone who thinks they are of no use. God will not argue with your beliefs.

# Change Your Soil

*"Surround yourself with people who have the same values as you, not those with the same interests as you."* Andy Stanley

Look around and take inventory of your life. Who are your closest associates? What books are they reading? What movies are they watching? Do they complain more than they create? The answers to these questions are a clue to your potential future success. People with the same interests congregate. People with the same values create. I agree with pastor Andy Stanley when he advises to find people who have the same values you do. People who share values produce differently from those who share interests. Our interest may put us in the same room, but it is our values that connect us. We both may be interested in going out and having a fun time. However, my values prompt me to go home to my wife. A fun time for me was drinks and dinner; for you it may be sleeping around with many women. We have the same interests, but our values separate us. I value family while you are simply interested in a good time. You must find people who connect with your values. Storms and droughts may come, but values keep you planted in good soil. The seed God planted in you will not grow in bad soil. What is good soil? Good soil is any environment that allows a seed to flourish. A seed is the most powerful thing in the world. However, without the right environment it is useless. A healthy environment is so important that God created it prior to creating humankind. God created a garden called Earth and planted seeds called humans. In fact, you are the only seed God gave the ability to plant itself. The environment you plant yourself in plays a vital role in your growth process. Your environment is essential to your growth. Everything soars in the right environment. Look at the importance Jesus places on environment in Matthew 13:1-9:

*That same day Jesus went out of the house and sat by the lake. Such large crowds gathered around him that he got into a boat and sat in it, while all the people stood on the shore. Then he told them many things in parables, saying: "A farmer went out to sow his seed. As he was scattering the seed, some fell along the path, and the birds came and ate it up. Some fell on rocky places, where it did not have much soil. It sprang up quickly, because the soil was shallow. ⁶ But when the sun came up, the plants were scorched, and they withered because they had no root. Other seed fell among thorns, which grew up and choked the plants. Still other seed fell on good soil, where it produced a crop—a hundred, sixty or thirty times what was sown. Whoever has ears, let them hear."*

In the parable, the soil changes, not the seed. The emphasis is placed on the soil, but too many people focus on the seed. In another part of the Bible Jesus compares faith to a mustard seed. The seed only produces in good soil or the right environment. The seed has the power, but it must be connected to the right environment to grow. Soil determines the growth of the seed. You are no different. Faith alone is not enough. It is where you plant or invest your faith that matters. You can be incredibly wise, gifted, or talented, but if you are in the wrong environment it will not matter. If you place your seed/dream in the wrong soil, it will never grow. Your soil is equivalent to your environment. Your environment is largely determined by your relationships. Your relationships will either kill or water your seed. If you are not growing, then it is time to evaluate your relationships.

You cannot be successful if you cannot gather support for your vision. Your vision will not survive on its own. You need the proper attitude to support your vision. Why? Because, your attitude plays a huge role in your ability to build relationships. People tend to trust you more if they like you. God wants to send people your way to help you with the vision. For this to happen, you must be a person who can work with others . Have you ever met someone—a naturally gifted person—but you were afraid to approach them because of his or her attitude? Do you remember how that felt? Good! Don't become that person. I learned early in my speaking career that the more people like you, the more they looked forward to listening to you.

I am not talking about spending all of your energy trying to get people to like you. I am saying that you should spend some time on yourself working to become likeable. You will never change what's around you until you change what is within you.

# Multiply and Grow

*Be fruitful and multiply.* Genesis 1:22

I parked my detective vehicle behind the church and prepared to enjoy my lunch. Eating lunch behind the church had become part of my daily routine. I wanted to be alone and out of the office. Each day, I noticed a group of Middle Easterners walking behind the church near the woods. As a police officer, I thought this was strange. My mind immediately went to the worst-case scenario. Were they hiding bodies? Smuggling drugs? But when I looked closer, I saw they were walking to a dry patch of land. They brought with them shovels, rakes, and gardening tools. It was then I realized they were just tending to a garden. One day, my curiosity got the best of me, and I stopped a woman and asked what they were planting. She smiled and said, "We are not planting, we are preparing the soil. Another group plants." I nodded my head as if I understood. The lady continued to the garden. I sat in my car and wondered why they worked the soil and another group did the planting. Why didn't the same people plant as those who worked the soil? Months later, sure enough, another group came and began planting and digging. I decided to ask someone why the groups worked separately. The guy looked at me and gave me the same smile as the woman. It was as if they took pride in sharing their wisdom with me. The man replied, "We don't work separately. We work with God. When we plant, God grows." Huh? He still didn't answer my question of why they did it in separate groups. So, I asked again. He replied, "Not separate, together!" My Western mindset did not allow me to grasp what he was saying. What I saw as separate actions were really one action in stages. The groups didn't see themselves doing different work. They saw themselves as doing God's work as a team. They saw it as their job to create a space for God to provide. Although they had different tasks, they all had the same mission.

It is our job to create something with our lives. Your life is proof that God wants you to be successful, but you must find your field and cultivate it. This means you must honor hard work. My whole life changed once I learned that God would not do all the work for me. I grew up in a church being told that God will do everything, and all I had to do was pray to Him. However, no one told me that God would not fight my battles for me but will fight alongside me. I wanted God's help in my life but was unwilling to fight. I had to learn to fight. You, too, must find a fight that invites God into the battle. However, your fight must be God's battle and not your own. The first and most difficult step is a relatively obvious and simple one: getting up. Life's job is to knock you down. If you don't get up, you lose. You will get knocked down. I REPEAT: you will get knocked down! But you must GET UP if you are to succeed. Notice that I didn't say survive, because truth be told, you can survive lying down.

Being comfortable is your worst enemy. Some people spend their whole existence striving for an easy life. This life does not exist. It takes courage to live this life. Every day, people commit spiritual suicide by deciding to lie down and let life just happen around them. When God places you in an area it is because God wants you to transform that space. You must be like the people behind the church. You must prepare a place for God to bless.

# Create a Space for God to Occupy

David did not stay idle while waiting to become king.

Don't wait for your dream to materialize. You must create your dream. As a motivational speaker, I needed to motivate depressed people. This was not as difficult as it may sound, because depressed people were all around me, but they were not going to come and just throw themselves at my feet. I had to make myself available to them. I had to find creative ways to let the world know I was here and available to them. One way I did this was by giving advice any time I had the opportunity. I began with my coworkers, strangers, and anyone who would listen. Then, I began to create an organization, like Hands Off, which dealt with abused children. I even started an empowerment coaching company called Wiseguy and gave free coaching lessons. I wasn't concerned about money; I was focused on finding my audience. Notice that I said audience, not money. My focus was *people* and not *things*. Success comes from people and not things. If you are going to be better, you will have to find a way to make the world (people) better.

I began to use my job as a testing ground. Before this, I hated going to court. I hated being the center of attention in a crowded courtroom. But now I turned the courtroom into my audience. I would testify about my cases as if I were on a stage giving a motivational speech. I worked to captivate the jury every time I opened my mouth, as I would engage their senses and spirits. Judges would turn around and look at me while I was testifying. I would look into the crowd and see people fixated on every word I spoke. At one point, I became the defense attorney's worst witness. Their goal went from keeping me on the stand to getting me off the stand as soon as possible. I had become a threat to their case. I was motivating the jury to convict their client. I spoke at every event possible. I didn't care about pay. I taught classes to nurses, visited group homes, and went to school during career days. It did not matter to whom; I just wanted to speak. I would go to restaurants, order food, and start a conversation and speak loudly so everyone could hear me. Everywhere I went, I transformed it into a motivational speaking event. This was a big step for a boy who grew up being made fun of because of the way he spoke. Growing up, I ran from crowds and avoided people. Now I was seeking them out.

I was becoming more confident in my speaking ability. In addition, I had just obtained my Master of Divinity Degree in Biblical Studies from The Interdenominational Theologica Seminary located in Atlanta, Georgia.

I was now hopeful that I could continue to improve my speaking by ministering in the church. The church placed me in training and started getting me prepared for ministry. My life was changing. I was excited, because no one had ever validated me for anything. It was nice to be recognized as someone with a gift that could change people's lives. I was told to be at a meeting with my elder and bring my resume. Once at the meeting, my pastor stood up and told the elder my desire to become a minister in the CME church. He told her that my resume was in front of her. I noticed the elder never looked at the resume. She responded by saying I would have to wait a year to even be considered for ministry in the church. I was upset and was ready to give up on the notion of becoming a minister.

Three weeks later I had an opportunity to meet the regional Bishop who was in charge of appointing ministers. I expressed to him my desire to become a minister. I informed him I had just graduated from seminary at the top of my class.

He glanced at me, smiled, and told me that I had still not put in enough time serving the church. I would have to wait years before he considered giving me a ministerial position. He told me to get back with him in a couple of years, and perhaps then he would consider giving me a part-time position at one of his smaller churches. I shook my head in agreement to hide my disappointment. I put my ego in check and saw this as an opportunity to help people. I knew people who had been waiting on a ministry position in the same church for years. I knew I would be no different.

I made a decision not to wait. I could not sit idly by and do nothing. The following week, I decided to order a microphone and some CDs. I was going to record motivational messages and give them away. I downloaded a sermon filing system on my computer and began preparing talks. I knew if I waited a year to accept a position, it would still be on their terms. But if I worked my butt off to improve my speaking skills and at the same time prepare sermons, then by the time they offered me the position, I would be in a better place, ready to succeed. I would have developed a name for myself, plus I would force myself to improve without needing permission. My goal was to change my position so that by the time they came to me and offered me a role, it would be on my terms. While I may have seen this as an obstacle, it was really a tool used by God to move me into purpose. I have come to learn that what often seems like obstacles are really instructions from God.

*"Obstacles are the part of the journey where God meets us to give further instructions."* Kevin McNeil

In the Bible, God only gives partial instructions. Moses is told to order Pharaoh to "Let my people go." Jesus only tells the disciples, "Follow me!" David is only told, "You are being anointed king." He is given no further instructions on how it will happen. He must trust God as he goes along. God only reveals more when David is willing to face insurmountable obstacles. The obstacles act as boundaries to further revelation. Goliath was not only an enemy for David, he was a path to the throne. It was a boundary David had to be willing to cross in order to get to the other side. Every promise of God requires crossing over a threshold. Israel had to cross the Egyptian border, the Red Sea, the Jordan River, Jericho and the occupants of the promise land. Jesus even had to deal with a cross. You must meet God at the cross. God will meet you at the crossing but you must do the walking.

God does not pay attention to man's boundaries. Like God, successful people break boundaries. If you look at history, you will discover most successful people broke the rules and surpassed established limits. The Wright Brothers broke boundaries. Steve Jobs broke boundaries. In fact, Jobs broke every rule in his field. When he was told that something was impossible, he sought to make it possible. I found this truth interesting. I have a lot of Christian friends. They complain and murmur far more than my secular friends. I must be honest: there were times I received more motivation from my secular friends than my Christian ones. They were the ones who told me to chase my dreams, keep believing in myself, and never give up. It was my Christian friends who often told me to wait, to persevere, and to live within my physical means. I had to stop listening to other people, Christian or Non-Christian, and take responsibility for my own life.

# CONCLUSION

## TAKE 100% RESPONSIBILITY FOR YOUR LIFE

*"And David was greatly distressed, for the people spoke of stoning him, because all the people were bitter in soul, each for his sons and daughters. But David strengthened himself in the LORD his God."* I Samuel 30:6 ESV

What do you do when all you have done is good, but things still turn out wrong? How do you find strength when you have done everything in your power to succeed and yet you still fail? What about the moments when you look up to heaven and ask God if He exists? We have all been there at some point in our lives. David was no different. At one point in David's life, he had been anointed king. He was on the run from Saul, who was attempting to kill him. And now, after fighting an intense battle with his men, David came back to an absolutely devastated camp. An enemy had destroyed everything. The wives of his people had been taken captive. On top of all of that, David's men wanted to kill him. He could have pitied for himself and blamed God for his failures. He could have said that life was not fair and that his haters were trying to destroy him, but he did none of those things. David had come to a point where he had to decide: Would he could give up, or would fight for what he believed in? However, do you know what David did? The Bible said he encouraged himself through the Lord. That's right! He took responsibility for what happened and went to God for answers. *"And David inquired of the Lord, "Shall I pursue after these enemies? Shall I overtake them?' HE answered, 'Pursue, for you shall surely overtake and shall surely rescue.'"* 1 Samuel 30: 8

David took responsibility for something in his life that wasn't even his fault. Yes, he was a victim, but he did not wallow in his pain, nor did he feel sorry for himself. David did not seek revenge, he sought justice. His thoughts were of his men and their wives. He took his mind off himself and focused on those who needed his help most. This is a great lesson the Bible teaches us about responsibility. My life belongs to me, no matter what happens to me. I cannot blame anyone else. Things will happen in my life, but it is **my** responsibility how I respond to them.

To be successful, you must take full responsibility for your life and what God has assigned you to accomplish while on Earth. No more complaining! I know this is hard for some people, but complaining will not solve your problems, and may even make matters worse. David's life was not perfect, but he took full responsibility for his mistakes, and full credit for his accomplishments. Life will not always be pleasant. Get over it! Live for your purpose and not for yourself, and you will discover that there are more happy days than sad ones. Decide that you are going to be successful and spend all of your energy and time going after your goals. My life changed when I stopped complaining about what was wrong with the world and began focusing on how I could fix a particular problem in it.

Maybe something happened to you in the past. I admit that it is hard to let go of bad things that have happened to you. I know this personally. I was kidnapped and sexually assaulted at the young age of twelve while walking home from school. A stranger forced me to do some horrible acts. This has haunted me all my life. It drove me to partake in dangerous and risky behavior. I had suicidal thoughts. I felt sorry for myself. I blamed God for not protecting me. I was acting as though I was murdered, but I still had a full life to live. Yes, I was brutally attacked and humiliated, but God allowed me to survive. And now I had to decide how I was going to live the rest of my life. I made the decision that I would use my experience to help other survivors of abuse overcome their shame, pain, and guilt. I have dedicated my whole life to inspiring people to live their best life. This book is part of that effort. It is my hope that you enjoyed reading it. I pray that this small book will make a big change in your life – after all, the little things can have the biggest impact.

Go to <u>Kevin-mcneil.mykajabi.com</u> to register for free Get Unstuck Course